AROUND THE WORLD
IN EIGHTY PLAYS

**Now regularly engaged as a Speaker, Brian
Freeland has, as theatre technician, stage
manager, lighting designer, playwright,
director, manager, producer or advisor
worked in forty-three different countries.
His journeys have included
eight tours of the Indian sub-continent
and two trips right 'Around the World'.**

ATWP

AROUND THE WORLD IN EIGHTY PLAYS

by

BRIAN FREELAND

ATWP

British Library Cataloguing-in-Publication Data
A catalogue record for this book is available on request from the
British Library

ISBN: 978-0-9934431-0-7

This edition first published by ATWP in 2015
and Printed in the UK by
CPI Group (UK) Ltd. Croydon CR0 4YY

This book is dedicated to those relatives, friends and
colleagues who have provided company in the good times,
and comfort in the not-so-good times. Thank you.

Chapters:

1. In Eastbourne with my grandparents.
2. In the driving seat.
3. In school uniform with Kenny Drew.
4. In Hong Kong
5. In The RAF.
6. In the cast of Eden End
7. In the Richelieu shop.

8. In the Desert.
9. In my Office in the National Theatre of Qatar.
10. In tights, in Nottingham
11. In need of a haircut.
12. In a Rolls-Royce with Taggart star James MacPherson, and the cast of The Boy Friend.

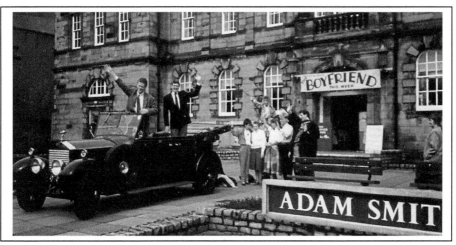

The River Charente

Introduction:

I started writing this book shortly after my sixtieth birthday. I still had plans for the future - some, admittedly, dependent on winning the lottery - but sixty felt like a good age to look back over a life that had taken me twice around the world and allowed me to work in forty-three different countries. A good age to recall some of the better things (and perhaps purge some of the less pleasant things) which had happened to me during those six decades. At that time I was in the Charente region of west central France, house-sitting for a couple who were planning to retire there. The duties were not arduous - mowing the lawn, weeding the borders, flushing bi-actif into the septic tank, cleaning the swimming pool and dealing with the contractors who - following some mysterious French contractor's timetable - would occasionally and unexpectedly return to continue re-roofing the barn or landscape the garden. Oh, yes - and feeding the cats. Zorro and Spot, two black and white kittens inherited from the previous owner of the house, and apparently convinced that I was there simply to do their bidding as and when required.

On one occasion, with the garden waterlogged following weeks of almost non-stop rain, I was trapped in the house. Radio Four's long-wave shipping forecast had warned us of westerly gales in sea area Biscay so I was well prepared and the storms provided me with an opportunity to complete the first draft of a script for a musical comedy. That done, and with the script already winging its way to London, the word processor was standing idle: I shut the kittens in the barn, opened a new file and typed BOOK at the top of the page.

Five years earlier I had put together my memories of tours abroad with various dance and drama companies in a talk entitled 'Around The World In Eighty Plays'. Several people were kind enough to say that the talk might provide the basis for a book. "*Nous verrons*" as the French say. "We'll see".

Ten chapters were completed before the garden dried out. Some of this material, detailing a trip down the River Charente from the source to Cognac, found its way into a monthly magazine The Scots Thistle.

Now, seventeen years later, I am back in France taking another tour along the River Charente; visiting old friends along the way, and giving a few talks to expat societies. Those ten chapters are in my briefcase. Will they be completed? Revised? Abandoned?

"*Nous verrons*".

Chapter One: From Chéronnac to Beckenham.

The house with the two kittens was in a little hamlet close to the town of Sauzé-Vaussais and not far from the River Charente, described by King Henri IV as "the most beautiful river in my kingdom". Not the longest, by any means. The fifth longest, in fact, at 371 kilometres and, although it gives its name to two of the French *départements*, Charente and Charente Maritime, it doesn't actually start in either of them. It has its beginnings in the little Haute-Vienne village of Chéronnac, on a plateau which must be almost floating on water since, within a few kilometres, it also provides the source of the Vayres (a tributary of the Vienne) as well as dozens of beautiful little lakes - some natural, some man-made.

There is a sign on the tiny bridge in Chéronnac's main street claiming '*Source de la Charente*', but the water under the bridge is already a small flowing stream. The sources (there are several of them) were, on my previous visit, clearly visible in a meadow about fifty metres further south, where the water literally bubbles up from the ground and eases its way down the slight slope, creating its own little valley in the process. From such humble origins begins the river which will eventually sweep under the huge curved arches of the impressive viaduct at Rochefort and out into the Atlantic.

However, those humble origins, those 'bubbles', are now hidden by hedges which separate the private gardens of newly-built houses from the small park developed by the Chéronnac Municipality between these gardens and the main street. In this park you now find mown lawns, sign boards and blue-painted seats designed to encourage visitors to their 'official' source of The Charente, a square, brutalist rock pool into which a hidden pipe slurps water in far greater quantities than any natural spring might be expected to supply; water which then runs in a man-made trench to join the original stream at the foot of the slope.

Chéronnac is not one of the great villages of France. On my earlier visit it had already lost most of its shops (in common with so many rural communities in both France and Britain) and one of its two bars. The post office had gone part-time, open only in the mornings. What stopped it being totally depressing was that the empty shops and bar had been cleverly converted into houses, with curtains and flowers in the windows - so that the village still felt lived-in, and alive. Now all signs have been removed from the Post Office, the hairdresser's shop next door has closed as has the bar opposite. The *Bar de la Source*, no less. Even if visitors find their way to the *faux-source*, they will not be able to celebrate with a drink in the local hostelry.

How often have we been warned not to return to any place where we once enjoyed happiness? I'm reminded of the Julian Slade/Dorothy Reynolds musical *Salad Days* when the young lovers sing "We said we'd never look back". I begin to wonder if this whole trip might prove to be a dreadful mistake. Will all those seventeen-year-old memories fit better into a waste paper basket than a glossy new paperback? Well, I'm here now: let's push on and see what happens.

From Chéronnac the embryo Charente heads off almost due north, as if anxious to get into 'home' territory as soon as possible. Within two or three kilometres it has been fed by other 'bubbling sources' and, walking along beside it, I find myself reminded of another little stream, the Ravensbourne, where Geoffrey Cleaver and I used to go fishing for sticklebacks. This wound its way through the southern parts of Bromley, then in Kent but now absorbed into Greater London, and the scene of my own humble origins.

Bromley is less than ten miles from central London, so the tiny Ravensbourne is a tributary of the mighty Thames, joining that river at Deptford Creek. More than that, it gave its name to our telephone exchange in those pre-digital days. Ravensbourne 0041 was the telephone number of our home in Queens Road, next door to Dunn's of Bromley. Dunn's sold furniture and furnishing fabrics, and had a large depository handling removals and storage.

They were also funeral directors, which was dad's job, and the reason why we lived next door. My parents only married in 1936, but this was already their third home. Their first was 4 Town Court Lane, Petts Wood, near the railway station and opposite open fields now occupied by a school. Dad was a driver (he got his driving license before driving tests were invented) and was also studying to become an embalmer with Dunn's funeral department; mum would help him with his revision in the evenings.

Our departure from Petts Wood was, so I'm told, quite dramatic: hearing the air raid sirens my parents grabbed me and my younger sister Valerie and headed for the garden only to be blown down the steps of the Anderson shelter by the bomb which fell behind them, destroying the house. Dunn's found us temporary accommodation, and then eventually moved us into the house next to their Queens Road depot. Bromley lies between the strategic wartime airfield at Biggin Hill and central London, and suffered quite heavily during the Blitz. Among other properties, eight of its churches were damaged or destroyed (five of them in one night), and I remember that Parish Church services were held in the Methodist church hall for several years.

On 16th April 1941 enemy action reduced the ancient Parish Church to a heap of rubble. Only the tower remained, still erect, but split from top to bottom. The church bells, dating from 1773, were so severely damaged as to necessitate their re-casting. Rebuilt, the tower now has a peal of eight bells and a tolling bell, as well as a plaque listing every vicar of the parish from 1223 to the present day.

Dressed in my scout's uniform I was part of the welcoming group of youth organisations greeting the (then) Princess Elizabeth when she attended the rededication service of that rebuilt Parish Church in October 1949. Other distinguished guests included the Lord Lieutenant of Kent, Lord Cornwallis; the Lord Bishop and the Archdeacon of Rochester; the High Sheriff, Mr Chamberlain (no, not that Mr Chamberlain); and Bromley's Member of Parliament, the Rt Hon Harold MacMillan with Lady Dorothy MacMillan. The newspaper reported that "The route from the church to the

Municipal Buildings was lined by Guides, Scouts, and local units of the Kent Yeomanry, Territorial Army, RAF Biggin Hill, Sea Cadets, Air Cadets, Army Cadets and the WRAC, together with the bands of the Home Guard Association and the Salvation Army".

I never met my father's parents. Grandfather William Jason Freeland had died in 1907, when my father was still only six years old. He had spent twenty-one "*straightforward, careful, honest and industrious*" years with the Pall Mall firm of Howell & James Limited who wrote "*we extremely regret that for family reasons he considers it advisable to resign his post*" in November 1901. Grandmother Caroline Maria (née Dennis) lived on until 1934, dying in the Pett's Wood house. My grandmother's aunt, Caroline Snatt, née Dennis, widow of the Eastbourne brewer Thomas Snatt, had opened a laundry business in Tideswell Road, Eastbourne. Following her death, grandfather William and grandmother Caroline Maria, nee Dennis, moved their eleven children from Balham back to their East Sussex roots and took over the management of the laundry. They may have had to borrow some money to cover this because grandfather's Will required the selling of their old Balham home to repay debts. One of the witnesses to the Will was Edward George Dunn, so there was already a family connection with my father's future employers.

I ought to know how and why dad became an undertaker, but I don't. It was often the case that the village builder was also the undertaker because he was the only one with suitable tools for the making of coffins, and a large-enough handcart to move the occupied coffins to their final resting place, but dad was never a village builder. It seems that his embalming studies only began when he started work at Dunn's, so perhaps he was driving hearses and learning the funeral business at the same time. He was certainly well respected within his profession, and was elected British Institute of Embalmers Chairman in 1948.

I should have asked Uncle Arthur about him, I suppose. Uncle Arthur (Hill) was my mother's brother, the last survivor of my parents' generation on either side of the family, and known to his many relations as The Godfather because, despite age and increasing infirmity, he had an encyclopaedic memory for family history. He never forgot a birthday or wedding anniversary, or the names of his many great-nieces and great-nephews in Britain and Australia. Too late now: beset by ill-health he said to his son "I'm glad I made it to 90, but I don't want to be 91", and he died a few weeks later. He was particularly proud of his diamond wedding anniversary telegram from the Queen, not least because two of his sisters had also achieved the same recognition.

Both our parents came from large families. Dad, Albert Freeland, the youngest of the eleven, lost two brothers in the first world war. They were in the Sussex Regiment, and their names are listed on the memorial in Eastbourne Town Hall. Another brother emigrated to Canada where he continued the Freeland farming tradition. Mum, Ivy Hill, was one of seven, and lost her youngest brother Ernie when he was killed outside Bayeux on the ninth day of the Normandy landings. We were evacuated near Gloucester at the time, and I remember dad arriving with the news (and with a newspaper cutting about him being 'killed in action' which we rediscovered among mum's papers after her death in 1989). My sister Valerie and I were sent out of the room, but I peeped round the door. Mum cried more that afternoon than at any time during the rest of her life.

That life cannot have been easy for my parents. I was born in 1938, the day before Hitler invaded Austria. Valerie arrived in 1939 soon after the start of the second world war, so mum and dad were faced with bringing up a young family under wartime conditions, with ration coupons for food and clothes, and the nightly fear of enemy bombers. Dad wasn't called up, perhaps because of his job, possibly because of his health, but he was an Air Raid Warden and often out at night on fire-watching duties. The shelter for that area was under Dunn's shop, and we spent many nights down there trying to sleep on the rough bunks with the sounds of sirens and fire engines and breaking glass coming from the streets above. Schools also suffered from the bombing which may be why we 'mixed infants' spent a couple of years clearly boarded out at a girls secondary school before moving on to Mason's Hill C of E Junior School just round the bend beyond Bromley South station. I can vividly remember the building and the playground and the awful outside toilets, but not the teachers - other than Miss Bishop (the teachers were all Miss or Mrs: there were no men). Miss Bishop was a tall thin greying lady who read us stories on Friday afternoons, perhaps setting down the foundations for my future theatrical career.

From Mason's Hill Junior School I won a scholarship to Beckenham Grammar School for Boys, involving a daily ride on the single-decker 227 bus. Usually with Kenny Drew, who lived just across from the Police Station and was in the same year. It was my only secondary school so I have no means of comparison with others, but it seemed more than adequate. A good general education with plenty of extra-curricular activities such as sport, music and drama. I was involved with house and school plays; there was a model railway club with its own layout, and a cinema club where I first saw *The Third Man*. The school also arranged a visit to Olivier's *Henry V* at a local cinema. With hindsight it seems to me that if you showed any aptitude for a subject or a sport then you were given every encouragement, but if you didn't then you were ignored no matter how great your interest or desire to learn. For instance, there was no playing field at Mason's Hill Junior, so I had no experience of team games. As soon as the masters realised this I was relegated to cross-country running (or cross-country ambling in my case) in the autumn (rugby) term, and sent off to play with a javelin in the cricket season after bowling just a single ball - the first time in my life that I had ever held a cricket ball or been on a pitch. I didn't think it was that wide, but Mr Champion was not impressed by my technique so that was the end of my cricket-playing career. Quite why someone who couldn't bowl a cricket ball should be trusted with a javelin I never dared to enquire. I don't blame Mr Champion. He had to organise house and school teams, and all in his own time. He was actually the Religious Education teacher, and a very good one too. His initials were R W, but he was known to the boys as Harry after the music hall singer Harry Champion (*Any Old Iron,* and *My Old Dutch*). One day in class he held up a letter from a parent and said "Strange how I keep getting letters addressed to Mr H Champion".

I was usually top of the class in maths. I don't claim any credit for this: I was certainly encouraged by an excellent maths master, Mr Hillman, but most of us are good at something and in my case it has always been mathematics. My mathematical logic also bluffed me through the science exams, though without much understanding or enthusiasm. I quite enjoyed French but struggled with German (probably too impatient to wait until the end of a sentence for the verb) and, I thought, did sufficiently well in English Language. I had not so far been permitted to study English Literature, but having now discovered theatre and cinema I was desperate to study arts in the sixth form. However the headmaster, Mr Wright, who had clearly been instructed to produce even more scientists, decided that my sixth form years would be devoted to Physics, Maths and Applied Maths. Playing with figures was fun for me, but I didn't want to do it day in, day out, for the next two years, with the prospect of a further three years at University. And anyway, things were tight at home as a result of dad's illness. It was time to get a job.

Chapter Two: From Lavaud to Pimlico.

It was the loss of a job and the chance of early retirement that took me to France in 1992. My contacts in the Ruffec area were very helpful in pointing me towards possible work opportunities within my area of experience, which at that time was in theatre and outdoor entertainment. One enquiry took me to a huge artificial lake with areas set aside for wind-surfing and water-skiing, for swimming, for fishing, for sailing and for nature reserves. The lake contained ten million cubic metres of water over an area of 225 hectares, and had been formed by building a barrage 20 metres high and 370 metres long across the River Charente, at a place no more than ten kilometres from its source at Chéronnac.

I went to look at the point where our little stream ran into this enormous lake. It was barely a metre across and perhaps half-a-metre deep: I found myself wondering what kind of genius could conceive a barrage 20 metres high and 370 metres long across such a tiny waterway. What happens to the rest of the river while this little dripping tap tries to fill a bath with ten million cubic metres of water? How do you convince potential financiers of the ability of this rivulet to maintain an investment of over 63 million francs (over £6 million)? Whatever the reservations, the *Barrage de Lavaud* opened in June 1989. I have to say that they got it about 90% right. For most of the summer the car parks are full, the cafe is busy, there are boats on the lake, swimmers in the water, sunbathers and fishermen around the shores. A superb outdoor leisure centre for the region, and a major holiday attraction but the summers can be long and hot and mostly dry. On that September visit seventeen years ago the lake was empty and deserted. Acres of sandy beaches but very little water. You could actually follow the course of the stream as it meandered across the sands and into the giant puddle below the barrage where, on my last visit, a heron had the fishing all to himself. Interestingly, you could walk all around the perimeter on the exposed sands, discovering on the way that there are a dozen more 'bubbling sources' feeding directly into the lake. Between them, they had that huge lake topped up in time for the next season's visitors.

Apart from the Ravensbourne, the nearest thing to a leisure lake in the Bromley area was Peter Pan's Pool at Catford. A little boating lake with an island, a cafe and a couple of small fairground roundabouts. The road past Peter Pan's Pool continued on to Lewisham where the little river Quaggy ran in a concrete gutter down the centre of the pavement alongside the main road before joining forces with the Ravensbourne.

Lewisham was dominated by Chiesman's Department Store which was, I believe, owned by relatives of the cricketer Sir Colin Cowdrey. Chiesman's has long gone, and vandals eventually caused the closure of Peter Pan's Pool. Youngsters have more sophisticated pleasures nowadays, but we certainly had our money's worth at both places. Messing about in boats at Catford provided an enjoyable summer outing (there was also a pet shop further along the road with a sad little zoo in the back garden) while Chiesman's was a part of Christmas with its animated window displays and Santa's grotto - although I personally preferred the giant model railway display at Gamages when finances permitted a family trip into the West End.

'We', by now, were five. Adrian had arrived in 1945, Ronald in 1948 and Jacqueline in 1952. Apart from our parentage we had little in common, and went on to develop very different characteristics and lifestyles, possibly because the gaps in our ages meant that we attended different schools and had our own circles of friends. There was never any money to spare: family holidays were usually on the south coast - sometimes in caravans, sometimes with dad's relatives at Eastbourne. Later, mum developed a passion for Old Time and Sequence dancing, and we swapped the caravans for holiday camps.

Dad spent a lot of time in his little workshop above Dunn's garage, making things for the home or toys for the children. He would say "there's another job jobbed" whenever he completed a project: a phrase I've often used myself. It can give a warm glow of satisfaction whether you have just re-roofed a barn or merely completed a mundane chore such as washing up. One of his more spectacular jobs in that tiny workshop was a pedal car for Adrian complete with a registration number AA123; AA representing Adrian's first attempt to say his own name. Dad's own vehicle at that time (he had several over the years, including a Norton motor-bike) was a Standard Nine, registration number KJ9062, which took us on many day trips and holidays, and once carried half my Scout patrol and their equipment to a weekend camp at Eynsford in the lovely Darent valley, near to Lullingstone Castle with its silkworm farm which provided fabric for several royal christenings.

As kids you are shielded from the realities of life. We always had enough to eat, were properly dressed and well educated. I don't doubt that our parents went without a great deal to make all this possible, but if there were problems they were never discussed with the children, or even discussed in our presence. We knew that dad was ill - he eventually went into hospital - and even when it was later explained that he had tuberculosis they never talked about the wider implications. He returned home for a while, but then had to go for an operation and a long period of recuperation at a sanatorium near Ashford, in Kent. Mum didn't drive (except from the back seat) so we were dependent on relatives and colleagues for hospital visits.

The illness interrupted dad's career: he had to leave Dunn's, and we had to leave Queens Road. Although obviously weaker and sometimes short of breath he was eventually able to return to work, and he joined the West Brompton firm of Ballards managing their 'parlour' (funeral directors are too posh to have shops). We lived above the parlour, first at the end of the King's Road in Fulham and then in Tachbrook Street, near Victoria Station. He was still an upright, imposing man and looked very smart in his undertaker's black, complete with top hat.

One of his prouder moments came when he was 'conducting' an important funeral with several following cars through Hammersmith Broadway during the rush hour. Traffic was blocked solid but he jumped out and, wearing his top hat and with rolled umbrella held high, cleared a way through the jam. On another occasion he was auditioned to take part in the television programme *What's My Line?* - his sole connection with show business. The production company subsequently decided not to pursue the idea. Wisely, I thought: although we had our family jokes about his work (it's a dead end job but it's a living: we live in the dead centre of town) he was particularly sensitive with his clients - the quick and the dead - and would have found it difficult to exploit potential humour in some of the questions. I suspect that his work may have given me a practical, even hard-hearted, attitude to death. It was always with us: in both Bromley and Pimlico his mortuary was in the house, and we got used to the presence of coffins and dead bodies. As a boy I would sometimes go with him to Trueloves in Sutton to collect a new supply of coffins, and I was amused rather than disturbed when he told me that the little metal flap at the end of an expanding tape measure could be hooked over the nail of the big toe when you measured the length of a corpse. Coffins were tailor-made: you ordered, for instance, a 5'10" by 19, with 19 inches being the width across the shoulders. It's probably all metric now. Funerals are certainly more expensive now: dad would be shocked and disappointed by the current costs of funerals, and the outrageous charges for cemetery space and services. Are you really better buried because you travelled to the church in a hearse the size of a bus? Or is it all a bit of a rip-off?

Chapter Three: From Suris to Fulham.

After squeezing through its 20 metre high barrage at Lavaud the River Charente is joined by the similarly-dammed Moulde, and together they tumble over a weir for their first brush with industry, the huge Delias furniture factory at Suris. At La Peruse the river shoots under the main Angoulême-Limoges road, heading north through gently rolling farming country - a beautiful drive on a sunny afternoon with poplars, alders and ash trees providing shelter both for the occasional motorist and the grazing cattle. The first obvious watermill is near Alloué, although the buildings have been converted into a private house with a well-tended garden. The mill wheel itself had been nicely restored, but was not operational. Just before the mill you passed a gleaming new wind generator on a metal tower. The times they are a-changing: that was the only wind generator on my first trip, now massive wind turbines are a common site in the French countryside.

At Chatain the Charente passes under what claims to be a Roman bridge: there may indeed be Roman foundations, but the bulk of the bridge dates from the thirteenth century and is no less attractive for that.

Close to the bridge is a marble monument with the inscription:

Chatain: Juin 1940-Mars 1943.
Ici la ligne de demarcation coupant La France en deux.
Homage aux patriots que, au peril de leur vie, ont su aider ceux qui l'ont forcée.

Near the junction with the River Transom, our river sneaks across the border into the *departement de la Vienne.* It shyly skirts around Charroux, which is a major mistake as this attractive little town is well worth a visit. There is an interesting medieval covered market in the town centre, but the most distinctive feature is the octagonal Tower of Charlemagne, all that remains of the Benedictine Abbey said to have been founded by the Emperor Charlemagne. In the early thirteenth century the Abbey controlled two hundred religious establishments, and even owned property in England. Up to thirty thousand pilgrims came each June to see the seventy relics which were said to include a morsel of the True Cross, and the 'Saint Prepuce'. The Abbey's nave was 120 metres in length, only four metres shorter than the Notre Dame in Paris, and its statues were compared to those in the cathedrals at Amiens and Rheims.

The Abbey was host to the 989AD Council of the Peace of God, when bishops from Bordeaux, Angouleme, Poitiers, Saintes, Perigueux and Limoges met to oppose those who "menaced innocent victims of war and their possessions". Burnt and pillaged during the Wars of Religion, and then demolished under the Revolution, the ruined Abbey was put up for sale in 1790 but happily bought by the village priest. There is now a concerted effort to preserve what remains of one of the most prestigious monuments of Roman France.

Charroux.

The friendly little bar just opposite what remains of Charlemagne's Tower was host, during my return visit, to the launch party for the first of what promises to be a bi-annual event - the Charroux Literary Festival. I hope to be over there promoting this book at the 2017 Festival.

Unconcerned by all this our river has swung west, passing the Chaffaud caves at Savigné, a prehistoric settlement where, in 1834, bones engraved with representations of reindeer were discovered. No shyness in Civray - the Charente runs boldly right through the centre of the town, even providing an island which houses the town's open air swimming pool. It is here that the Charente comes of age; its playing days are over and it has become a working river. It enters Civray through one mill, a large four-storey building that almost blocks the road to the campsite, and leaves through another, a more attractive building in a rural setting.

Civray is best known perhaps for the 12th century Church of St Nicholas with its colourful painted interior, and its carved light stone frontage depicting angels, virgins (both wise and foolish), the signs of the Zodiac, and St Nicholas himself saving three girls. The town has about 3000 inhabitants, and is at its busiest on Tuesdays and Fridays - market days. I used to have a stall at the Tuesday market selling British produce: customers included both the resident British with a yearning for marmite or custard powder, and those French who appreciate that our teas, marmalades and chocolate biscuits are immeasurably better than the local equivalents. And as there is no local equivalent for lemon curd, peanut butter or salt & vinegar crisps, they would make their way to my draughty corner of the market square each Tuesday morning.

The nearest market to our new home above the Fulham funeral parlour was just a short walk away, in the North End Road. Stalls all down one side of a long narrow street which still managed to function as one of the main traffic arteries of the borough. When we moved to Fulham in 1953 I was only a few months away from GCE 'O' levels, and the education authorities agreed that I could continue at Beckenham Grammar. This meant a daily ride on the dreaded number 11 bus to Victoria and then a train to Kent House station. There was a scheduled service which got me to school with only four minutes to spare before Assembly so, if the bus was delayed - either held up by traffic or simply waiting for its colleagues (the number 11s preferred to travel in convoy) - I would be late. Punishment was an hour's detention after school supervised by the deputy head, a Spanish teacher with Denis Healey eyebrows.

Finishing the fifth year with six 'O' level passes, and having decided not to stay on for a 'scientific' sixth form, it was time to find a job. I was accepted by Fulham Borough Council as a junior accounts assistant in the Borough Treasurer's Department, and started work at the Town Hall in the summer of 1954. The duties were not onerous - making tea, ordering stationery, stamping outgoing mail, that sort of thing - but then the salary wasn't over-generous at only £2.40 a week. When my new colleagues discovered that I wasn't entirely without brains they allowed me to undertake some of their more menial tasks. Thanks to Mr Povey I began to learn about PAYE and National Insurance, and the building trade's holiday stamp scheme. Sitting at the next desk was Alan Saunders, a young and newly-married worrier from Wolverhampton who had the unenviable task of preparing all of the Council's incoming invoices for payment. They had to be rubber-stamped, signed by at least three officers, numbered, collated, and entered by hand into the relevant account books. Once a month he would stagger off to the Finance Committee with his boxes of invoices, nervous that a councillor would find a mistake or query a payment. Three minutes later he would be back again, the accounts having been passed 'on the nod', and his impending breakdown was delayed for another month.

Mr Jordan, the Borough Treasurer, and his deputy Mr Craven kept fatherly eyes on me, and encouraged me to start a book-keeping course two evenings a week at Westminster College of Commerce (using the dreaded number 11 bus again). Incidentally, I was told that 'book-keeping' is the only word in the English language with three consecutive double letters - if you discount the hyphen. I hope that this information, if true, will prove useful to you. The course was enjoyable, and I passed the Royal Society of Arts examinations, parts 1, 2 and Finals, within two years. That was essential - there would be no third year. At the age of eighteen I was eligible for National Service.

The most important event in those two years had nothing to do with accounts or local government. In 1955, for the first time in their history, Chelsea Football Club won the League Division One Championship. Their ground, Stamford Bridge, was about two hundred yards from the Town Hall, and I had started supporting them soon after our move to the Kings Road. They had a strong team. Several were England internationals - one, the left half Saunders, as an unpaid amateur. His professional colleagues were on £15 a week - although it was alleged that managers sometimes dropped some cash into an amateur's boot after a match. Chelsea's professionals included Peter Sillett and Stan Willemse as full-backs; Ken Armstrong was a creative right half, Eric (Rabbit) Parsons and young Frank Blunstone were the wingers. If they had a 'star' then it was centre forward Roy Bentley, who would surely have played more often for England had Jackie Milburn and Stan Mortenson not been around at the same time. There was never any trouble at football matches in those days. In that Championship year they had enormous crowds (75,000 for the top of the table clash with Wolverhampton Wanderers) and children would be passed over their heads to sit inside the fence so that they could see the game. I remember Roy Bentley lobbing a goal over the head of the Wolves goal-keeper Bert Williams from somewhere near the halfway touchline flag, quite as exciting as any of David Beckham's efforts, but without the publicity afforded by multiple replays on the television screen.

As often as possible we would travel to away matches, once enduring an all-night coach ride in the snow to see Chelsea lose an FA Cup match at West Hartlepool. We reassured ourselves on the way back that this would leave the team free to concentrate on winning the League which, greatly to our surprise, they did. That Championship was the peak of the team's achievements. They never looked like winning anything else so, when they sold Bentley to nearby Fulham Football Club I followed him to Craven Cottage. There was always a happy atmosphere in that little ground on the north bank of the Thames, possibly because the chairman at that time was variety star Tommy Trinder. His teams included the incredible Johnny Haynes (capable of opening up any defence with an accurate diagonal pass), the future England manager Bobby Robson, future TV pundit Jimmy Hill, England's 1966 World Cup-winning full back George Cohen (another undertaker), and the prematurely-balding genius of Eddie Lowe at left half. Their forays into the (then) First Division never lasted long, but they had some good cup runs - including an FA Cup Final at Wembley.

Around this time I also developed an interest in cricket - watching rather than playing, thanks to R W (Harry) Champion. Both Lords and the Oval were within easy reach of Fulham, and I spent happy days at both grounds. Abiding memories of 1955 include a twenty-four-year-old Brian Close opening the innings with Jack Ikin against South Africa at The Oval, top scoring with 32, and Denis Compton scoring 150 out of the Middlesex total of 206 in the annual Bank Holiday match against Sussex at Lords. In the second innings he scored 2.

The start of work and the evenings at night school meant the end of my connections with the Scout movement. I had transferred to a troupe at Fulham Broadway, and was fortunate to be one of a handful of London scouts selected to work at the Coronation of Queen Elizabeth II. A large tented village had been set up in Hyde Park for the thousands of police drafted into the capital for the event, and we worked with them for about three days - mostly on kitchen duties, serving food and washing up. Our reward was a place alongside the police inside the crowd-barriers in Park Lane, with an uncluttered view of the passing procession and a packed lunch identical to those issued to the policemen. It was magnificent, despite the rain which had threatened to spoil the big day. The Queen and the Duke of Edinburgh were in the gold State Coach, with other members of the Royal Family and dozens of foreign monarchs and presidents following in other coaches and cars. The one who made the greatest impression on the crowds was a very large, very jolly lady, Queen Salote of Tonga, who insisted on riding with the roof of her coach wide open exposing herself and her tiny, morning-suited companion to the elements. When asked who this diminutive gentleman was, Noel Coward reportedly replied "her lunch!"

Chapter Four: From Battles to Bristol.

The French language is a cocktail with three main ingredients: *Gallic-Celtic* dating from pre-Roman times; *Latin* - the written language of Gaul during the Roman occupation, and the *Germanic* of the Franks tribe which over-ran the country at the end of the fifth century. This makes it quite difficult for historians to determine the origin of place names: in the fourth century the poet Ausone (310-394) wrote of the river *Carantonus*, but this is believed to be a Latinisation of the Celtic word *Carentonna*. River translates into French as *un fleuve* or *une riviere*, but the Charente is definitely *un fleuve* as it is not a tributary to any other river. The French word *ville* (town) comes from the Latin *villa*, a large country house or farm with lots of live-in servants or slaves, while the most popular name for French kings derives from the Germanic Chlodwig, who was the first Christian king of the Franks. This was softened to Clovis by some, and to Ludwig by others, eventually becoming Louis. Chlodwig's name for his new kingdom was Frankenreich. I don't know about you, but I think I prefer King Louis of France to King Chlodwig of Frankenreich.

A period of relative quiet under the Franks was interrupted in 732AD when Abd-al-Rahman led thousands of Arab soldiers from southern Spain and North Africa up through the Charente region. There was a huge battle in the area between Tours and Poitiers, and the Arabs were decisively beaten by forces led by Charles Martel (Charles the Hammer). Despite the rout, some of the Arabs settled in this area as indicated by village names such as *Les Sarrazins* (the Saracens) and *Les Negres* (the Moors). Charlemagne passed through the area in 777AD, founding the Abbeys at Charroux and Nanteuil, and it was probably the enormous wealth stored in these two abbeys which attracted the next invasion, only this time the threat actually came up the River Charente itself. These days the river is only navigable from Angouleme to the sea, but in 844 the Vikings were able to drag their long, shallow boats upstream under cover of darkness from their base somewhere near Cognac. They passed the next couple of years doing what they did best - raping and pillaging - before retreating towards Bordeaux.

The next army to come raping and pillaging through the region was - would you believe - the English. Eleanor of Aquitaine had inherited most of south-west France - greater in area than the land controlled by the French king. She divorced Louis VII, and when she married the Plantagenet King Henry II in 1154 he automatically became Duke of Aquitaine. The hamlet of Fief Richard and the town of Montjohn are almost certainly named after two of their sons, the Princes Richard (the Lionheart) and John who both enjoyed the French lifestyle. As did their troops, who hit the bottle and let off some of their aggression in the local towns.

Life in the British forces in the late 1950s was unlikely to be as exciting. Among my Christmas cards at the end of 1956 was a buff envelope marked OHMS, my call-up papers for National Service in the RAF: two years that would change my life. Basic training - square-bashing - was done at Bridgnorth, conveniently close to Wolverhampton where Jimmy Mullen and Bert Williams were still playing for the Wanderers. The trips to Molineux ate heavily into our weekly pay of twenty-eight shillings (£1.40), but we saw some great football and it got us out of camp for a few hours.

We had missed the Suez crisis by several months, and our National Service coincided with a period of relative peace throughout the world so I can't therefore thrill you with reports of my battlefield exploits, my meetings with Montgomery, or my extensive tours with ENSA. My most terrifying experience happened during a weekend guarding Halfpenny Green, a disused wartime airfield. There were four of us, with an NCO, and we took turns to patrol the empty buildings. I'm still not sure what we were looking for. Left-over Nazis, perhaps? I had the dawn patrol, and went out in thick fog armed with a rifle. No ammunition - just a rifle. It was so foggy that the entire airfield could have been over-run by insurgents during the night without anyone knowing, and I was nervously struggling to see anything through the gloom. Suddenly I made out a figure - about six feet tall with one arm raised. I lifted my empty rifle, moved forward, and challenged..... a petrol pump!

At that time the RAF was looking for interpreters and, thanks to my O-level in French, I was offered a place on a training course - in Mandarin Chinese. This involved spending the best part of a year at Pucklechurch, a training camp just outside Bristol, studying Chinese five-and-a-half days a week, with occasional time off for football, scrumpi and, a relatively new experience for me, professional theatre.

Towards the end of my fifth year at school I had been cast as a policeman in the school play, *Who Killed The Count?* Even at fifteen I was already six feet tall, with size ten shoes. The annual school play was a usually a classic - Shaw or Shakespeare - but in 1954 they decided to do a thriller. Officially, it was an attempt to boost ticket sales, although I've always considered it another element in the headmaster's deliberate policy to steer me away from English literature.

Mick Brown, a fellow student on the Chinese course, had done some amateur acting prior to National Service, and together we went to see the Bristol Old Vic's production of Bernard Shaw's *Man and Superman* performed in the beautiful old Theatre Royal. Denis Carey was the director, and the leading man was a young, exciting and supremely talented Peter O'Toole I was hooked right from the moment of his first entrance, which he seemed to start from the stage door (some three floors down from the stage at the Theatre Royal) getting louder and angrier until he finally burst through the door upstage centre. Wow! What an entrance. The rest of the evening was equally captivating, and we caught all of his performances throughout that season (including Vladimir in *Waiting For Godot*, the title role in *Mother Goose*, and a flat-footed Archangel Gabriel in the French playwright Jean Giradoux's *Sodom and Gomorrah*. We also saw most of the plays presented at the Little Theatre, up in the roof of the Colston Hall, as well as several touring productions at the Hippodrome. The latter included a visit by Dame Flora Robson and Andrew Cruikshank on a post-London tour of The House By The Lake, a nice-enough play but lost in the vast expanses of the Hippodrome.

I much preferred the intimacy of the Little Theatre with its repertory company, the Rapier Players, run for 28 years by the husband-and-wife team of Robert Russell and Peggy Ann Wood. They took it over in 1935 as a weekly rep, kept it going throughout the war, and switched to fortnightly in 1949

- all without any subsidy. If they were working on a shoe-string it didn't show: I still remember the atmospheric sets and lighting for an excellent production of *The Rainmaker*. These evenings made a pleasant break from the endless studies, and were to prove the start of a lifetime in professional entertainment although I didn't realise it at the time. Until then my only contact with live theatre had been an occasional family outing to a Christmas show. I do vaguely remember sitting in the back row of the upper circle at Streatham Hill Theatre to see *Where The Rainbow Ends* starring Anton Dolin. At a Penge Empire panto I first realised that characters appearing in a stage performance could speak directly to a live audience, and I remember seeing Arthur Askey in pantomime at Croydon - which would have been my first experience of the Bee Song. He was at his best in pantomime, and I enjoyed one of his last outings as Dame, with Dickie Henderson junior at Nottingham Royal in 1972.

In Bristol the routines of service life continued: we still had to box up our blankets every morning at the head of the bed, and polish the billet floor every Tuesday evening, but we made the most of whatever free time was available. Football now meant Bristol Rovers at nearby Eastville, although we did cross the city once when Tottenham Hotspurs were Bristol City's visitors at Ashton Gate. I don't think it was a cup match, so it must have been a charity game - perhaps a benefit. Ted Ditchburn was in goal for Spurs.

We must occasionally have gone to the Odeon or Gaumont, but the cinema that still stands out in my memory was a little fleapit, probably long-since demolished, just around the corner from the bus stop. The Tatler, perhaps? Can't be sure; it was a long time ago. It was the sort of cinema that often turned to soft-porn movies in a last desperate attempt to stay in business, but at that time it was still screening genuine art movies, many of them from the continent. We saw *The Fiends* there - can anyone ever forget the first time they saw that 'dead' body get out of the bath? - and an incredible double bill that coupled Brigitte Bardot in *And Woman Was Created* with *Quatermass And The Pit.*

Somehow, in amongst all of this, Mick and I found time to get involved with a local amateur drama group, the Tudor Players, who had the use of a church hall in - I suspect - Tudor Road. I forget how this came about - either we saw one of their productions and got chatting to them afterwards, or they had advertised for new members (amateur groups, whether dramatic or musical, are invariably short of men). We helped out with the play that was already in rehearsal and then, as our time in Bristol was drawing to an end, we were both cast in a thriller - Janet Green's *Murder Mistaken*. Mick played Edward Bear, a gentleman who had the nasty habit of killing off his wives for their money - and I, inevitably, was the policeman who eventually arrested him. Business was good, although I suspect that we had some 'comps' in for the Saturday matinee as a lady near the front kept shouting out warnings to the about-to-be-murdered wife.

We were only with them for a short time, but were made most welcome. One couple, Beryl and Don Philpotts, remained friends for many years afterwards. I tried to visit them whenever my work took me to Bristol, and we exchanged Christmas cards and occasional letters. Don was a research scientist with WD & HO Wills, the cigarette manufacturers and one of Bristol's major employers. They kept me up-to-date with theatrical life in the city, and with the progress of their children Chris and Jean through school and college, but we sadly lost touch during one of my foreign trips.

Almost certainly my fault: it must be very difficult to follow my many changes of address, or even my many changes of country. Letters go astray; addresses are lost. You can't carry everything with you on a long foreign tour, but I should have made a greater effort to maintain contact with people who have been so important in my life. If the Philpotts or other discarded friends are reading this - my apologies!

Chapter Five: From St Macoux to Hong Kong.

When you move home, especially to another country, the sadness of leaving old friends behind is partly balanced by the pleasure of developing new friendships. The Hapels, for instance: Christine and Francois and their three sons. Francois is a woodworker, a specialist in the intricate art of marquetry with commissions from as far away as Paris for the restoration of antiques. He has diplomas for his work in "preserving the national heritage", one of only seven or eight Frenchmen sharing that distinction, and was also much in demand as a teacher of marquetry. Originally from Le Havre, he and Christine settled in the village of Brux in the Vienne, where Francois set up his workshop. Later they took over an adjoining building, formerly a restaurant, and fitted it out as a 'mini-market', a corner shop/general store. Christine gave up her job in the *Marie*, and negotiated a contract with the supermarket chain Intermarché for the supply of groceries and dry goods at trade price, to which they added seafood, bottled gas, flowers and - following our meeting at Civray market - a British Food Corner.

I was able to help with supplies and with introductions to potential suppliers, and spent two crazy days chasing around England introducing Francois to Hanley Glass and China in Stoke, Cottage Delight preserves and sauces in Leek, stationery and Far East imports in west London, fancy goods in Bognor, and Bookers food wholesalers in Portsmouth. He filled his van with goodies like a schoolboy let loose in a sweetie factory and, a few months later, took Christine on a return trip. The transport costs meant that these purchases were unlikely to offer much in the way of profit, but they certainly made the shop look more attractive and brought in a wider clientele. Eventually, of course, the strength of the pound removed any chance of profit on the British goods while the supermarket competition made the whole venture uneconomical. Christine, with three growing boys to look after, found herself tied to the shop for six-and-a-half days a week with ever-decreasing profit margins. At the end of 1999, they took the decision to close down and, revelling in their new-found leisure, Francois started teaching marquetry in Poitiers, and Christine did a full-time business management course. The oldest and happiest student on the course.

For a couple of years I was *'papi anglais'* (English grandfather) to their three children, and did my best to remember birthdays and other family events. I was invited to the confirmation and first communion of eldest son Nicholas, and hospital-visited when David fell out of a lime tree. David was accident-prone: only a few weeks previously he had cut his foot open on broken glass while fishing in the river at Brux. Vincent, the youngest was then eight, and developing his own personality after growing up in the shadow of his elder brothers. Like all French kids they were able to switch in an instant from the formality of greeting a visitor with a polite handshake to arguing with a foot-stamping, arm-waving intensity that would be considered 'overacting' on any British stage. We spent one happy Sunday afternoon lazing (as far as one can laze in the company of three energetic, noisy lads) on the banks of the Charente near St Macoux. Francois was swimming (the river is too narrow there for his favourite sport, wind-surfing); Nicholas and David were fishing. Nicholas presented me with his catch to take home for my dinner: despite his enthusiasm for the sport he didn't like the taste of fish.

Between Civray and St Macoux the river has left the *Vienne* and returned to its own *département*, now heading south towards Ruffec. At St Saviol it passes the enormous Lescaux factory where they make butter and cheese, and from which in times past an evil-looking effluent would emerge to float down-stream until halted by a water-mill. Most of the millponds have barriers which wind up and down to control the flow of water, and many years ago I met the man who had the job of cleaning the surface of the millponds by lowering these gates a few centimetres and sending the effluent on its way - until brought to a halt again at the next barrier. Apart from patches of weeds the water at St Macoux is now clean enough for the youngsters to play in: it seems that either technological improvements or ecological pressures have solved the effluent problem as the river at St Macoux is now crystal clear.

As was the water in Hong Kong's New Wave Bay, except during the monsoon. After a year of wall-to-wall Chinese lessons the time came to leave Bristol and in early 1958 we flew out to our new base on the eastern end of Hong Kong island. Naturally, as a loyal member of the Royal Air Force, and a child of the Blitz whose family had donated the railings from their front garden to help build Spitfires and Hurricanes, I expected to make the journey in an RAF plane. But no: my first-ever flight was aboard a BOAC Argonaut.

In my memory this trip seems to have happened mostly at night. We re-fuelled in Rome before flying on to Iraq where we spent the night in the Shat-al-Arab Hotel in Basrah. You can imagine what a group of young British airmen made of that name. Expecting some hostility we had been ordered to travel in civvies in the hope that no-one would guess we thirty young men with short-back-and-sides haircuts were servicemen. I suspect, however, that we might have given the game away by checking into the hotel carrying our grey RAF-issue kit-bags with name, rank and number stencilled on the side. After dinner some of us walked into the town, shocked at our first sight of soldiers - of our own age, if not younger - patrolling the streets with rifles slung over their shoulders. There was open hostility towards us - so different from the friendliness and hospitality that I would later find in some other Arab countries - and we soon beat a retreat back to the hotel. Another stop saw the Argonaut refuelling at Patna in north-east India. Even at night the heat and humidity were overwhelming, but that didn't stop us enjoying an ad hoc football match on the runway against some of the airport staff and local youngsters. It's strange; I've toured throughout India many times since then but have never been back to Patna. At least, not yet.

The arrival in Hong Kong, flying into the old Kai Tak airport, was one of the unforgettable experiences of a lifetime. There is little I can add to the many existing descriptions except to confirm the spectacular first view of the Colony (as it then was) with its mountains and bright green paddy fields, the blue waters of the harbour alive with junks and ferry boats (Hong Kong is Cantonese for 'beautiful harbour'), and the myriad buildings crowded right down to the waterfront. The Argonaut flew in low over the city, apparently heading straight for a mountain, before banking to starboard and gliding in over a main street. We could see right into buildings each side of us, and were aware of flashing lights below holding up the traffic while we passed overhead. Then, suddenly, we were on the ground, landing on a runway which ended at the water's edge.

When we arrived, in 1958, work had already started on another runway. From our barracks on Small Wave Bay just across the harbour we were able to follow its progress. A couple of mountains were being demolished and the rocks used to build a promontory straight out into the harbour. Over a mile long, and wide enough for a main runway plus the taxi lane. Wind direction permitting, the approach to the airport would now be made over the eastern harbour, making life safer and quieter for the people of Kowloon. We had our first sight of Britain's new jet plane, the Comet, when - in BOAC colours - it made the inaugural flight onto the completed runway, having recently beaten America's Boeing as the first commercial jet plane to carry passengers across the Atlantic. Happily it landed safely, but this was not always the case: the occasional flight would miss, or would run over the edge of the promontory. Once we heard that this had happened to an American Air Force plane: whether that was true or not I never discovered, but even the thought of it gave us RAF men a little glow of pleasure.

The then Colony of Hong Kong was a very different place to the Hong Kong which was reluctantly handed over to China in 1997. In 1958 there were only three multi-storied buildings - hardly tall enough to justify the title skyscraper - on the entire island, and they were along one side of the cricket ground right in the city centre. I'm fairly certain that all three were banks, and therefore of little interest to Junior Technicians (as we now were) on National Service pay. We were more interested in the water-front bars, many with live music, all with live girls (expensive) and local Tiger beer (cheaper than the imported brands). Our favourite was Old Toby's Bar, which had a good traditional jazz trio and some attractive and friendly hostesses. Friendly, that is, until the wealthier American or Australian servicemen arrived, when we would be left with our beer and our music. Fair enough - business is business. If I seem to dwell on our relative penury it is with some justification. Hong Kong was a bustling, lively place with plenty to see and do - if you could afford it. Cinemas, theatres, beaches, restaurants - including the famous floating restaurants in Aberdeen harbour on the south of the island - were all available, as were trips up into the New Territories or the ferry across to Macau, but they were for the most part the stuff of dreams. Even the journey from Small Wave Bay into the city was a problem: we were dependent on lifts or finding enough guys willing to share the cost of a taxi. We did sometimes stay in town overnight, at the cheap but efficient China Fleet Club just near the ferry terminal.

Nowadays there is new airport on the largely-reclaimed island of Chek Lap Kok: tunnels connect the airport, Kowloon and Hong Kong island. In 1958 Star Ferries provided the only cross-harbour link. There was also a main line railway running from Kowloon station up through the New Territories to the Chinese border. Today it will take you all the way to Guangzhou (Canton) and beyond, passing the site of the 1958 barbed wire and guard-posts.

I did occasionally escape up into the rural peace of the New Territories. Hills, paddy fields and solitude, disturbed only by our four Hawker Hunters patrolling the border and putting the fear of God into eight hundred million communist Chinese. Some days we had only two or three of these in service, which might have provided some small measure of reassurance for the 'opposition'. My oddest experience in the New Territories was finding a bar in the paddy fields, well away from any habitation. A simple wooden hut with a counter, two small square wooden tables and four chairs inside, and a battered metal Guinness advert on the outside. A hand-painted sign over the door said "The Better 'Ole".

The work was mostly routine, sometimes interesting, and only occasionally exciting. The boredom of service life was partly relieved by the opening of a camp cinema, the Astra (someone translated the RAF motto *Per Ardua Ad Astra* as "it's hard to get into the Astra"), and we had a good sports field on reclaimed land below the camp with football and hockey pitches. Mick Brown, the amateur actor from Bristol, and his mate John Gulvin were both skilful hockey players, and I had played a bit at Beckenham Grammar (we did hockey in the spring term): we all three made the station team, but hockey wasn't popular and, if I'm honest, there was little competition for places. There was no beach in Small Wave Bay, but some good swimming off the rocks. We had an Ayah who did our laundry and starched our wide khaki shorts, and a visiting tailor would make and mend. The weather was pretty good outside of the monsoon season, and life - on the whole - was rather pleasant for a group of young men most of whom were away from home for the first time. Of course, there were the usual tribulations of service life; the RAF Police (Snowdrops) who expected you back in camp before midnight, and the NCOs insistent on socks being pulled right up (we wore long khaki socks with our flared shorts), and hats worn straight. And the endless memos and notices: my favourite read "It should be noted that the ration of eggs on this station is one egg per airman per head per day". Only fair, I suppose, for all those airmen with more than one head, and on a par with a sign I saw recently in a motorway service station undergoing renovations. "We apologise for any inconvenience caused by these improvements"!

Chapter Six: From Rom to the London Palladium

You can't travel far in France without being made aware of the sufferings caused by the Nazi occupation of this lovely country. Talk to any elderly Frenchwoman and she will have her own stories of the hardships; running businesses, farms and homes without the men who had been shipped away to work as slave labour or forced into the camps, enduring hunger and poverty while the occupying forces helped themselves to the food and the accommodation.

The demarcation line between Occupied France and the part controlled by the Vichy government of Marshall Petain ran east of the town of Ruffec whose inhabitants had to get special permits to cross the 'border'. The Resistance (the *Maquis*) was very strong in this region, and it was perhaps to link up with them that a dozen British and American soldiers parachuted into the woods a few days after the Normandy landings. They were captured and shot (in contravention of the Geneva convention) and are buried in their own little 'war cemetery' in a corner of the churchyard at Rom, a village a few miles north of Ruffec. There was certainly plenty of resistance activity in the region, and an enormous memorial to the French Resistance now stands on the hill above Chasseneuil. Many years ago I spent a fascinating afternoon at Melle with a former *Maquis* leader, Guy Bourdet, a teenager at the time of the occupation (all the men of working age had been transported). He had been in regular radio contact with England, and had even - foolishly, perhaps, given the obvious danger to himself and his colleagues - kept transcripts of all the radio communications, which he showed me. At the end of the war, this teenager accepted the surrender of the local German garrison, locked them in a barn, and took away their boots. "To stop them running away?" I enquired. "No" he replied, "we needed boots; we didn't have any".

One sad aspect of the occupation was to end a chapter of history on our the River Charente. The flat-bottomed, single-masted sailing barges, *gabarres*, had been ferrying cargo on the lower Charente throughout the nineteenth century but, this trade had declined with the arrival of the railways and the last working *gabarre* sailed from Jarnac in 1930. The Nazis, preparing for the planned invasion of Britain, rounded up all the remaining barges and towed them to St Nazaire, where they were discovered and destroyed by RAF bombers. Fifteen years later, in January 1959, this same RAF flew me home from Hong Kong via Changi airport in Singapore, for demobilisation and a return to civilian life at the end of my two years of National Service. Fulham Borough Council was obliged to find me a job if I wanted to go back, but I explained to Messrs Jordan and Craven that the two years away had left me with altered aspirations. "Such as?" they wanted to know, and I found it difficult to answer. The year in Bristol had given me a love of theatre which has never left me, and the tour of duty in Hong Kong had opened my eyes to the possibilities of travel, and of living abroad. What I sought was a job that would combine the two.

What I actually got was a job as Trainee Manager at the London Palladium. They wanted someone with accountancy training to help with box office figures and salaries. I offered my RSA certificates in book-keeping and the massive experience gained from two years as Junior Accounts Clerk at Fulham Town Hall, and was accepted. I was back in an office again, but an office in one of the most famous theatres in the world, home of variety, pantomime and the television show *Sunday Night At The London Palladium*.

Earlier in the century most towns had at least one theatre; many had two or more. Some would house resident repertory companies, but the others depended on touring productions, amateur operatic societies and pantomime. They were defined as Number Ones, Twos or Threes depending on their seating capacity and the quality of their facilities: the number one circuit included the major venues such as Bristol Hippodrome, Leeds Grand, Birmingham Hippodrome, Liverpool Empire, Manchester Palace and the Kings Theatre, Glasgow as well as many others long since demolished or transformed into cinemas, supermarkets or television studios.

By the beginning of the fifties most of the main venues were under the control of two managements, Moss Empires and Stoll Theatres, but with the increasing popularity of cinema and the development of television their business was declining. Cissie Williams, booking manager for Moss Empires, could no longer afford to send out tours of *Oklahoma* and the like, with full chorus and orchestra, and would settle for yet another cut-down revival of *The Desert Song* or girlie-shows such as *'Nudes Of The World'*. In those days carefully posed nudity was permitted, but the girls were not allowed to move.

The two managements still retained their London 'flagship' venues. Stoll had the Coliseum, Moss had the Hippodrome, the Victoria Palace and the Palladium, but even in London the situation was changing. Both managements invested heavily in commercial television; the Coliseum had a few good years left but would eventually be sold to English National Opera. The Hippodrome was transformed into a theatre restaurant, The Talk Of The Town, with some of the world's biggest stars appearing in cabaret (the only, unforgettable, time I ever saw Judy Garland live was at The Talk Of The Town). Later, under the management of Peter Stringfellow, it became London's biggest discotheque. A later management was forced to close when they lost their drinks license, and the building is currently a Casino.

The London Palladium had long been known as 'the home of variety' but really hit the headlines when they imported bill-toppers from America. Danny Kaye had been an instant success, attracting return visits from members of the Royal

Family: Johnnie Ray's female fans packed Argyle Street and refused to go home until he sang to them from the Palladium balcony. The television series Sunday Night At The London Palladium capitalised on this formula, using top international stars to headline a bill that always included a team of dancers, a game show, and a regular host.

For the first few series the host was comedian Tommy Trinder, one of only a handful of comics with a genuine talent for ad-libbing and the ability to quieten hecklers with a quick riposte. I once saw him stop his act for an interruption which he sensed rather than heard. "What did you say?" he enquired, and was told "You heard". "I didn't", said Trinder, "or you'd have had your answer by now". His most famous show at the Palladium was one that didn't happen - or, to be exact, one that started nearly two hours late. Something went wrong with the link from the theatre to the television studios where they would be recording and relaying the live Sunday night show. While the technicians worked to find and repair the fault, Tommy Trinder entertained the packed theatre for ninety minutes, totally unscripted, and deservedly received a standing ovation. Almost immediately he was back on stage to host the live TV programme. A few years later I would witness this talent at close quarters. I was stage managing a charity show at the old Metropolitan, Edgware Road with Tommy as top of the bill following Michael Allport and Jennifer, a magic act involving dozens of different coloured doves. As each dove miraculously 'appeared' Jennifer would take it from Michael and put it on a large bird- stand at one side of the stage.

Whether she moved the stand in the process or a slight breeze caught the curtains we were never sure but, as these curtains closed for the end of their spot, they toppled the stand, and frightened doves took flight to all parts of the theatre. Happily we had the right man for the crisis, and Tommy spent the next half-hour ad-libbing the recovery of the birds. It was probably even funnier than his prepared act.

By the time I arrived at the Palladium in February 1959 the big American stars were moving into cabaret, and Tommy had handed over the Sunday Night show to Bruce Forsyth. They still did a big expensive pantomime every Christmas, but the variety seasons were now built around British artistes. Singer Frankie Vaughan topped the bill for the spring show, and Max Bygraves headlined the summer revue with three large, energetic American singers, The Peters Sisters.

I suspect that our ancient sign-writer at the Palladium scribbled his notes on the back of a cigarette packet in the pub. Once, when Max Bygraves was off sick for a few nights during the summer show he provided a sign for the foyer which read "The management is delighted to announce that, owing to the indisposition of Max Bygraves, tonight's performance will star.....". That was hastily redone; as was the huge poster on the rear of the building advertising a forthcoming West End production of *The World of Suzy Wong*. In place of Gary Raymond, the classical actor booked to play the male lead, our sign-writer had painted Paul Raymond, king of the Soho strip clubs.

And that was the beginning of my professional theatre career; Trainee Manager at the London Palladium. When I tell you that one of my trainers, the Box Office Manager, was arrested for embezzlement, you'll see that my training was in perfectly safe hands. Don't ask me what he did or how he did it: I know, but I'm not telling. I may need to try it myself one day.

Chapter Seven: From Vouléme to the Victoria Palace.

We left our river above the weir at St Macoux. I explained earlier that historians find it difficult to determine the origin of place names because of the mixture of ancient languages involved, but there is general agreement that the St Macoux of this Charente village was the same man who gave his name to the town (and ferry port) of St Malo in Britanny. They certainly got around, those saints.

The section south of St Macoux is one of my favourite stretches of the River Charente. It divides in two to pass under the bridges at Vouléme where you will find some painted wooden angels in the charming twelfth century church. Alongside the church Mme Marie-France Vergnaud (now long- retired) ruled over the packed lunchtime tables of a friendly little inn. We celebrated my sixtieth birthday with lunch there, and when Marie-France realised the significance of the occasion she added six candles to the delicious cherry tart she had prepared for dessert. She did a mouth-watering *maigret de canard*, although you had to ignore the fact that your meal was probably related to the friendly ducks waddling around her river-side garden.

Mme Vergnaud's charming little French riverside hostelry is currently called Edna's, and painted in bright blue and yellow. If that doesn't upset the locals, then the signs and menus printed first in English and then in French might just do the trick. Although there is acceptance that the influx of British expatriates, mostly pensioners, has benefited the local economy, a degree of insensitivity towards their hosts occasionally apparent.

Next stop down the river is Condac, the first of several places on the river with a name ending in *-ac*. We shall be passing Montignac, Fléac and Jarnac - and stopping off for a drink in Cognac - so I enquired about the derivation of this common suffix. John Walker, author of the excellent guide book *All About The Ruffecois* told me that it comes from the Latin genitive *-iacus*, which usually translates as "at the place of". He said that the suffixes *-ay*, *-e* and *-ecq* are all from the same source. The French have obviously followed on from this tradition since *chez* (as in *Chez Branger* or *Chez Fouche*, two local villages) also means "at the house of ....."

In 1897 a huge Roman cemetery was unearthed at Condac indicating that the Romans probably made their base in the valley around the river crossing, rather than up the hill where the important market town of Ruffec now stands. *Le Moulin Enchanté* (The Enchanted Mill) at Condac is a commercial operation which seems to have lost its enchantment. I remember it as having a busy restaurant, a discotheque, mini-golf and boats for hire - the first place, I believe, since the great lake at Lavaud where you could go 'messing about on the river', and it was here on Good Friday 1442, during a lull in the 100 Years War, that Charles VII and his son, the future Louis XI, did exactly that. Unfortunately they capsized and, according to a contemporary report, "*were tossed into the clear waters as much in danger of drowning as the meanest of their subjects, which could have provided an early end to the line of Valois*".

The next mill downstream is at Rejallant where there is a large canoe club, so perhaps this very British pastime of messing about in boats is finally catching on. Some twenty-five years ago the authorities decided to develop the facilities at Rejallant and advertised for a manager. One of the perks was a little flat in the old mill building (where the huge waterwheel had been restored and could sometimes be seen in operation). It was suggested that I apply and, from an original short list of fifteen, I was one of two (the other being a Frenchman) called back for a second interview. He got the job - and the flat. Nothing much happened there for two or three years, but Rejallant has developed and is now very busy during the summer months with swimmers in the millpond, canoeists below the weir, and fishermen everywhere. The cafe/restaurant has been enlarged and modernised in a manner which would certainly outrage British preservationists, but despite that (and the restaurant's vastly increased prices) it still remains a most pleasant spot to pass a warm summer afternoon.

Vouléme Church   *l'Aire de Rejallant*

It was a cold winter morning when I first climbed the marble steps and passed through the front doors of the London Palladium. At that time the Palladium pantomimes often continued until Easter, and the publicity each side of the doors was for the 1958/59 production, *The Sleeping Beauty.* The all-star cast included Charlie Drake and Thelma Ruby as the King and Queen, Edmund Hockridge as the Prince, Bruce Forsyth as the Knave, and Bernard Bresslaw as the Captain of the Guard. Managements were starting to book artistes on the strength of their television reputations: Charlie Drake had his own series, Bruce Forsyth was compere of Sunday Night at the London Palladium, and Bernard Bresslaw co-starred in a series called The Army Game.

The spectacular new scenery (by Edward Delany and Tod Kingman) had designs largely based on playing cards, and the end of Act One had the whole Palace of Cards collapsing.

The one line that sticks in my memory came just after the prince's arrival and the kiss that awakens the sleeping princess. The entire court was still asleep, covered in massive cobwebs. The King woke first and, walking around looking at the sleeping bodies, said "It's like doing a midnight matinee in an Ovaltine factory". Robert St John Roper was responsible for the magnificent costumes, and the entire production would move on to another venue the following Christmas with the script adapted to suit whichever stars were in favour - or in a television series. In the mid-1960s that same Sleeping Beauty turned up at the Theatre Royal, Nottingham with some tired-looking scenery, and a totally different cast of refugees from television.

The Palladium was often chosen as the venue for prestige charitable events such as the Royal Variety Show or a Night Of A Hundred Stars. They were hard work for everyone but made a break from the routine of a longish run, and often attracted artistes who would not normally be available to us. Singer Eddie Fisher appeared in one of these, I remember, with his then wife Elizabeth Taylor watching from the box. A young Tommy Steele was also in the line-up. His wife Anne, arriving for the rehearsals with Lionel Bart, took one look at the miles of brass handrails in the foyer and said "Imagine cleaning that lot every morning".

Another of these charity shows, at the Prince of Wales Theatre, should have featured two of my great comedy heroes, George Burns and Gracie Allen, but Gracie was too ill to travel (she sadly died shortly afterwards). However, Jack Benny was also in the cast: he donned the frock and stood in for Gracie. Burns and Allen became Burns and Benny, for one night only. It was hilarious - and I was there to see it. These were pre-terrorist days: security was less of a problem than now, and we had every confidence in the police cover provided for these Royal events. So much so that when an assistant rushed into the office saying "we've just had a telephone call; there's a bomb in the Royal Box" our manager George Margrave responded "Well then, if I were you, I should stay well away from the Royal Box".

He was a respected, experienced and popular manager: I only saw him hesitate once, when someone reported to us that two pairs of feet could be seen under one of the cubicle doors in the gents toilets. We followed him gravely to the basement, wondering how he would handle this. He knocked on the cubicle door which was eventually opened to reveal our elderly commissionaire sitting down enjoying a cigarette - with his shoes off. That same commissionaire was sent with a message to ATV Headquarters, and was totally overwhelmed by the experience. "They have music everywhere" he reported, "even in the lift!"

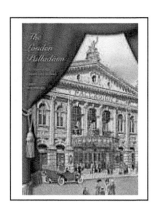 

The Crazy Gang had recently opened their penultimate show *Clown Jewels* at the Victoria Palace, but appeared in one of our charity events with the highlight of act two, their fabulous 'Disappointed Debs' routine. Only a few weeks prior to the show's opening it had been announced that debutantes would no longer be presented to Her Majesty at the annual Queen Charlotte's Ball, and the Gang appeared, dressed up to the nines, as five woebegone young (well, youngish) ladies singing of their disappointment.

One verse went:

> *My three feathers with much flair*
> *I stuck firmly in my hair*
> *They say I can't make my bow;*
> *Where shall I stick my feathers now?*

Their stage shows were not for the prudish but were fun - and flexible enough to accommodate the unexpected. One night Bud Flanagan announced that Sophie Tucker was in the audience, and tried to coax her up on stage. She feigned reluctance only until her musical director Ted Shapiro had edged his way into the orchestra pit, at which point she made her way on to the stage and gave us a heart-warming, and apparently impromptu, rendition of *Some Of These Days*.

The Gang once engaged Denis Carey from the Bristol Old Vic to direct them in the Pyramus & Thisbe scene from Shakespeare's *A Midsummer Night's Dream*, which they played "absolutely straight". Well, almost straight: the wall did have "We Want Watneys" painted on the back but, as Bud explained to the audience, "we get a free crate of beer every night for showing that".

Chapter Eight: From Vertueil to Butlins

If you are looking for a guide to the Chateaux of France then you have come to the wrong book, and the wrong river. Try the Loire or the Vienne. The Charente is farming country, and the architecture is built around farms, farming villages, and market towns. There is, however, one chateau, one that is impossible to ignore. Sitting high above the river Charente, overshadowing the interesting little town below, is the magnificent *Chateau de Vertueil*. It is owned by members of the La Rochfoucauld family, a family known to have entertained both the Emperor Charles V and King Henri XIII. The original building dates from the 11th century, although there are many later additions. It was plundered during the Revolution, and some priceless tapestries cut up into squares by the farmers and used to cover their potato clamps in the winter. Recovered and restored, these tapestries are now in the Metropolitan Museum of Art in New York.

Seventeen years ago, according to my brief-case chapters, the chateau had a single occupant, the last of the dynasty, elderly and in ill-health. It was understood that the local Council was even then preparing for his demise, and for the anticipated rush of visitors that would follow any public opening of the Chateau. Plans were well in hand for the construction of car parks and toilets, and the positioning of access signs, so there was an added frisson as I approached the town. What would I discover?

Well, I discovered that the declining recluse had struggled on for a further two years before finally passing on, and that the family had, indeed, considered selling the Chateau. However, to the dismay of most of the population of Verteuil, two younger members of the family decided to move in, and the best laid plans of mice, men and the Verteuil municipality were put back in the drawer for at least another generation.

In times past we had several enjoyable evenings at La Paloma, a pleasant restaurant with an attractive open air terrace in a quiet *impasse* to the east of Verteuil but, as with so many other small businesses, it has struggled over the years. I discovered the shutters closed, and weeds growing in the car park: apparently the owner's wife left him, and he just locked up and walked away.

It is always a problem recommending favourite restaurants. Chefs move on or owners sell up or tastes change, and what was once a thriving business can quickly become an empty disaster. There is nothing sadder than a restaurant with all the tables laid, and no customers. It used to be the tradition in France that everyone ate out on Saturday evening and again *en famille* for Sunday lunch. Nowadays they shop in the supermarkets, eat at McDonalds or buy a take-away to nibble in front of the television. The small businesses which gave life to the town - the shops, the restaurants, the hotels - are disappearing in a welter of bankruptcies; the real town centre is now outside the town, a trading estate on the Ring Road.

Happily, the Marmite is still open. For the French a *marmite* is a large cooking pot, not a yeast extract, and the restaurant of this name sits on the right bank of the Charente as the river enters the town of Mansle. The collection of exotic birds housed in aviaries in the garden had disappeared, but the lunchtime tables were full. The uniforms of Police and Pompiers were evident among the diners. Eat where the locals eat is always a good rule, wherever you travel in the world. Mansle was important in Roman times and was still on the main route of traffic heading for Bordeaux and Spain until the Emperor Napoleon laid his sword across a map of the region to indicate the route of his proposed trunk road to facilitate the movement of his troops. The town is quieter now and worth a visit, especially the lower end of the town around the narrow bridge, where you'll find the parish church and town hall on your left, and the hotel on your right.

It was in another water-front hotel that I spent my first night in Wales. It was in mid-May, and certainly warm enough for picnics; possibly the warmest week of the summer. We had travelled up by train, crossing that incredible curved wooden viaduct at Barmouth, and were booked into a hotel in Criccieth preparing for our first day's work at Butlin's Pwllheli Holiday Camp. The camp would not open to the public for another week, during which time we prepared our various departments for the 6000 or so happy campers who would enter the gates each Saturday. As stage manager for one of the three theatres I hung curtains, overhauled the lighting equipment, decorated the dressing rooms, and helped the scenic artist who was already at work on the scenery needed for the four plays (two comedies, two thrillers) that we should be presenting in the Playhouse throughout the summer.

The other two stage managers (the camp had three theatres) had been there the previous summer and they helped me find my feet - this was, after all, the first time I had run a show on my own. At the Palladium I had kept my eyes open and not been afraid to ask questions. I knew how to run a flat and how to cleat scenery; I could focus a spotlight, and I had watched Johnny Badesi operate the impressive lighting control console at one side of the Palladium's Grand Circle. Not that we had many spotlights in Butlin's Playhouse, and the lighting control was very rudimentary - a far cry from the West End. Remember that I am writing about Butlins in 1960: the facilities have improved over the years and their theatres - the few that remain - are now capable of staging revues and variety of the highest standard.

Many performers learned their trade during these seasons at Butlins (Jimmy Tarbuck was our redcoat comic one summer) but it was also a superb training ground for the technicians. Two, sometimes three, shows a day ranging from professional Repertory and Variety companies to Redcoat

Revues or Old Time Music Hall or Minstrel Show, plus the Miss Butlin and Glamorous Granny and Talent Contests. Cabaret in the bars, a church service in the theatre on Sunday mornings, and visiting stars on Sunday evening. Each show had its different technical requirements, adding a bit more to my 'on the job' education.

My special favourites were the wet weather shows. The camps had a slogan "When it's wet it's always fine at Butlin's" and there was pressure on us to entertain the campers during inclement weather - something not entirely unknown on the north Wales coast. The call would go out - "wet weather show" - and all entertainment staff not involved on other duties would gather in the theatre where redcoat Duncan Menzies would try to organise some sort of presentation using the available talent. Duncan was director of the Redcoat Revue, superb in cabaret, and had been around for a few seasons. He had dozens of sketches and routines up his sleeve, but sometimes forgot that we didn't all share his experience. He would say something like "we'll do the vicars sketch next" and then rush on to make an announcement without stopping to find out whether anyone else had even seen the vicars sketch, let alone knew the words.

Once he said to me "Set the stage up like a French bistro, with tables and chairs, bottles and glasses, and get everyone on stage singing The Night They Invented Champagne while I go off and change, then I'll come on and do some French jokes". We did our best. A couple of tables, four or five chairs, a beer bottle or two and some dirty glasses from the dressing room. The curtains opened and the redcoats sang: *"The night they invented champagne - er - er lala lalalal lala lalalala ...."* Duncan re-appeared after his quick change into striped blazer and straw hat to find the entire cast and the audience, who had quickly realised that no-one knew the words, doubled up with laughter. We never did another French bistro scene.

Over the years I've met some great stars and some wonderful people (not always the same thing) but none more so than our resident top-of-the-bill at Pwllheli, Norman Evans, one of our greatest-ever pantomime dames. He was the most kind, charming, helpful man you could wish to meet, always finding time to discuss a problem or offer some advice, despite a serious illness which made even walking uncomfortable - although you wouldn't have known that to watch him on stage.

His 'Over The Garden Wall' sketch as a gossipy old woman was one of the classics of the music hall, but he was also an accomplished musician on both piano and trumpet: his piano routine was the model for later comics such as Les Dawson, and he shared the trumpet routine with a gentle little glove puppet. His lovely wife was never far away: nurse, driver, companion. They were such a happy couple it was a joy to see them together. She was an indispensible part of his puppet routine, hiding under the table so that at the end she could ease her hand into the discarded puppet which then waved goodbye to Norman as he left the stage. Despite these thousands of 'appearances' she had never actually been seen on stage so, on the last night of the season, we dressed her in men's clothes complete with cloth cap and, replacing a stage hand, she carried on a stool that Norman needed for the act. The twinkle in her eye, and the enormous smile from Norman as he realised who it was, were wonderful to see. The season ended in September: by November Norman was dead, and buried at Blackpool in a grave which had no tombstone, but a little brick edifice with the words 'Norman Evans' Last Garden Wall.

Saturday was change-over day at Butlins, with last week's campers leaving and the new ones arriving. A busy day for the Redcoats who liked to get an early look at the 'talent' as the coaches pulled in, but a quiet one in the Playhouse. A chance to go to the pub in Criccieth where everyone would sit quietly at ten o'clock, the official closing time, until the village bobby had finished his rounds. Then the singing would start. Full-blooded Cambrian harmonies, with at least half the pub fancying themselves as conductors, until Land Of My Fathers finally turned us all out into the Welsh night. Years later I would be sitting in another pub, in Warrington, listening to an old man talking to someone about his car. "I've been all round the world in that car" he said, "all round the world. Criccieth. Everywhere".

My last season with Butlins was spent at Ayr, on the west Scottish coast, and not too far from Glasgow. It wasn't the easiest of seasons - the Redcoat who was doing much of the comedy work in the stage shows and outdoor events was caught stealing from the camp shop and dismissed. This meant extra work for everyone else, and I was drafted into the Minstrel Show. I was also 'volunteered' to be the redcoat thrown from the high diving board by Captain Blood into 'Scotland's largest outdoor heated swimming pool'. I have to say that it didn't feel particularly warm at ten o'clock on a Tuesday morning but there were compensations. One of the films being shown throughout the season was *Seven Brides For Seven Brothers*, and no matter how busy things were I always found time to slip in at the back and watch Michael Kidd's choreography for that incredible barn-raising routine.

The director and co-star of our resident revue company was Glasgow-born Lee Young. His real name was Jimmy Young, but he changed it because of confusion with a singer whose record of Unchained Melody was doing well in the charts. Both of them went on to enjoy successful careers; Jimmy as a Radio Two presenter in London, and Lee as a director and performer in Australia. The last of the old-style Scottish comedians, Lex McLean, was presenting the summer season at Glasgow's Pavilion Theatre, with a complete change of programme every fortnight. So, every second Monday, Lee and I would drive into the city to catch the latest offering. Lex's shows were a mixture of the 'tartan' (kilted dancers and accordion players) and the downright blue. The accents were pretty formidable, and I often wished I had an interpreter so that I could appreciate the *double entendres* as quickly as the elderly ladies packed into the front rows. "Hey, Jimmy. D'ye ken whit's a spinster?" "Aye, she's a wiman wha's done wi'out being marrid". You'll have to translate that one for yourselves.

The sketches were a wonderful kaleidoscope of mistaken identities, like the nervous apprentice gigolo arriving at the wrong house for his first-ever engagement: the butler who greets him is actually expecting a vacuum cleaner salesman and tells the distraught would-be gigolo "Everyone's waiting for you in the drawing room. Madam says she can't wait to try out your Little Goblin on the sofa". The 'little goblins' were certainly kept busy at Pwllheli and Ayr. Even on that first night in the hotel at Criccieth one of the chalet maids grabbed me and said "Well, you get a reputation anyway working at Butlins; you may as well earn it. Come on". All part of my on-the-job experience.

Chapter Nine: From Montignac-sur-Charente to Paris

Autumn arrived in western France with a vengeance in 2001. The lawns, waterlogged after weeks of seemingly endless rain, were white with frost, and the winds had stripped the leaves from the trees. The chestnuts and walnuts had been gathered, and the hunting season had begun. Those countrymen who could hold a gun, and several who couldn't, went out every weekend accompanied by a strange assortment of dogs, and popped off at anything that moved. Cats are kept indoors, dogs have coloured kerchiefs tied around their necks in the hope that this will prevent them from being mistaken for foxes or rabbits. Deer and wild boar move discreetly to the inner recesses of the woodland, warned by the barking of the pseudo-hounds. The ducks suddenly disappear from the Charente about now, but whether they have been shot or merely gone into hiding is not clear. Despite the apparent popularity of this so-called sport I suspect that French hunters kill more animals with their cars than with their guns.

You can also tell the season from the publicity on walls and in shop windows. Posters for the first bingo sessions of the autumn (for prizes, not money) have replaced those for the *brocantes* (boot fairs) and race meetings. A choice of *brocantes* every summer weekend , but the racing is more sporadic and usually takes place in fields or meadows adapted for the event. There is, however, a excellent race track at Montignac-sur-Charente where an enterprising mayor managed to clear a large area of land next to the river with the intention of opening a huge sports park. Racecourse, tennis courts, swimming pool, etc. Much of the site remains empty but the racecourse was eventually completed: it hosts three successful evening meetings each year, a mixture of riding and trotting, with tote facilities, a bar and two restaurants. I went with friends Sue and Mervyn White to the autumn meeting and we set up our picnic table and cold-box alongside the home straight. A lovely, warm, sunny evening, fun company, some close-fought races, and a good meal. And Sue won 420 francs on the third race. A particularly pleasant way to pass a late August evening.

On the other side of the river - which now has a canoe slalom course - there is an excellent camp site. This suffered badly, like so many waterside sites, from the *tempete* - the hurricane which blew for several hours through the afternoon and night of December 27th 1999 and destroyed so many trees. Nationwide, they estimated that some 360 million trees were lost, and every region has its own story of the horrors and devastation. The garden of my 'house-sit' lost two giant walnut trees, one of which brought down part of the roof and guttering. The hamlet was cut off for several hours with fallen trees blocking every road, but by mid-afternoon on the 28th every village and farm had some access to a main road: not always the most obvious route, but access. It took several weeks to clear some of the lanes, and every day you could hear the sound of chainsaws (including mine) clearing routes and cutting up fallen trees. We were four days without electricity, and ten days without a telephone.

It was raining when I returned to Montignac, so I nipped into the Taillefer Restaurant for lunch. It was Ascension Day, a public holiday - although the greengrocer had still set up his regular Thursday stall under the brand new Market Hall which fills most of the square in front of the restaurant. A restaurant named after Guillaume Taillefer (literally *William Cut-Iron*) who was a huge hero in local folk-lore. He was given this surname when, after an unresolved battle against the Normans, it was agreed that Guillaume and the Norman king, Storin, would fight single-handed. With one blow of his sword Guillaume Taillefer split in two not just King Storin, but his breastplate as well.

Around 1020 AD one of his descendants, the fourth Count Guillaume Taillefer, undertook to build a castle on the precipice at Montignac, overlooking the river valley. A century later Count Vulgrin II Taillefer, added the Donjon, the "high, strong tower surrounded by solid walls" parts of which still stand today dominating the town and the important junction below where the bridge connects with the main north-south highway. Incidentally, another Taillefer descendant was Minstrel to William the Conqueror during the 1066 Norman invasion.

The 1776 installation of locks on the river encouraged new businesses to start up in Montignac. An early mayor, Dr Feuillet, built the town hall and schools, and developed the two squares. A later mayor tried to talk me into re-opening the little hotel facing the Donjon, and backing onto the river. At the time, with his sports complex strapped for cash and with no plans for completion, it didn't seem such a good idea, but I'd often wondered whether or not I made the right decision. With lunch eaten, and the rain stopped, it was time to find out.

The hotel frontage on the main square has been turned into a private house. The rear section facing the river has been replaced by a newly-built town house in light stone, with a riverside garden (*photo*). Very attractive, very desirable - and the right decision. I still have good feelings about Montignac-sur-Charente, but I now accept that the town didn't need a hotel. Especially mine. If you do visit Montignac (and I recommend the race nights) take a look at the stunning old mill building, a former felt factory, sitting astride the river: now there's a property that really would make a superb hotel.

Timing is all important whether you are opening a hotel or changing jobs, and I certainly got lucky when I returned to London at the end of my third Butlins season.

Simmy Levenstein, the lively little chief electrician at the Comedy Theatre, offered me a job as assistant electrician and lighting control operator just at the time when theatre lighting was going through its biggest change since the invention of electricity. Until then, stage lighting had been very 'flat' - long metal battens containing a row of ordinary light bulbs. Three or four hanging above the stage without another metal trough providing the footlights. These bulbs were usually split into three circuits, each with a different coloured filter. Shape, the third dimension, had to be contrived by painting shadows onto the flat canvas scenery, and by the use of heavy make-up on the faces of the performers.

The mass manufacture of individual spotlights made them cheap enough to hang all around the stage and auditorium: light coming from several angles illuminates natural shapes. Actors no longer need to plaster their faces with greasepaint: two spotlights from the front (from different angles) push forward the nose and delineate the eyes and the cheekbones. A third spot from behind shapes the shoulders, and the back of the head. Makes them three-dimensional. Canvas flats were replaced with three-dimensional scenery - allowing Sean Kenny to become famous overnight for his chunky, lumbering sets for the musical 'Oliver'.

Strand Electric led the way in Britain with the invention of the remote control panels (based originally on the Compton organ console) with 120 or more tiny faders feeding through low voltage cables to the bank of 240watt dimmers hidden away at the back of the building, or under the stage (we're talking about the early sixties: everything is digital now - so I'm told). For the first time one man could control all of these circuits, and from a position where he had a good view of the stage - ideally at the rear of the auditorium. The Comedy Theatre was installing such a control desk as I arrived, and I received on-the-job training from the people who had designed and installed it.

Most West End theatres were operating at this time with a mixture of full-time and part-time technicians, known respectively as daymen and showmen. The showmen usually had other jobs and were often unavailable for mid-week matinees: stand-ins were recruited from other theatres. In this way I managed to work on three different shows at the same time: our own production of *A Passage To India* with a large cast led by Zia Moyeddin, Norman Wooland and Dilys Hamlet for six evenings plus matinees on Wednesdays and Saturdays, alongside Thursday matinees of *Flower Drum Song* at the Hippodrome and Tuesday matinees of *Irma La Douce* at the Lyric (with Shani Wallis and Gary Raymond).

A few months later the Royal Shakespeare Company adopted the Aldwych Theatre as its London base. They added a forestage to take the actors closer to the audience, and improved the sound and lighting installations. Their new lighting console was identical to the one I was using at the Comedy - and they were looking for an operator. Simmy Levenstein, bless him, suggested that I should apply. His opposite number at the Aldwych, Johnny Beaumont (another of nature's gentlemen) took me on, and I was sitting at the lighting control when the Aldwych re-opened in December 1960.

The Director, and the brains behind the idea of a London home for the RSC, was Peter Hall, and I remember him saying at the first press conference that he hoped they would never prove that Bacon wrote Shakespeare's plays as he had no interest in running the Royal Bacon Company. Michael Blakemore, no great fan of Mr Hall, wrote in his book *Stage Blood* that he never heard Peter tell a joke. I'm not sure if that one qualifies as a joke or not. He may not have had a sense of humour, but Peter Hall knew his way around a boardroom. When he arrived at Stratford the RSC was still operating in the black: he pointed out that they would never get public funding that way, and quickly ran them into debt.

Hall had gathered together a superb ensemble, many of them direct from the season just ended at Stratford - and several of them on long-term contracts (I believe that this was the first time in British theatre that actors were contracted for longer than a season). Peggy Ashcroft was the *Duchess Of Malfi*, alongside Max Adrian, Eric Porter and Derek Godfrey; Richard Johnson and Dorothy Tutin starred in *The Devils* (an adaptation by John Whiting of Huxley's book The Devils Of Loudun, but more of this later); Eric Porter had the title role in Anouilh's *Becket*, with Christopher Plummer as the King.

Dorothy Tutin was Viola in our first Shakespeare, *Twelfth Night*, with Derek Godfrey as Orsino, Max Adrian as Feste, and a cross-gartered Eric Porter as Malvolio. Miss Tutin also co-starred with Ian Holm in *Troilus And Cressida* set in designer Leslie Hurry's infamous sandpit (the critic who thought the sand was sawdust should have been around to shovel it into barrels at the end of the show). Vanessa Redgrave battled with Derek Godfrey in *The Taming Of The Shrew*, and was coyly romantic with Ian Bannen in *As You Like It*.

One of the reasons for the addition of a London venue for the Royal Shakempany was to give the actors a break from Elizabethan costume dramas. To this end Michel St Denis directed a stark *Cherry Orchard*, with John Gielgud and Judi Dench joining the resident company; and there was a brave attempt at Brecht's *Caucasian Chalk Circle*, directed by William Gaskill (until the actors began to panic about the amount of time being spent on 'improvisations', at which point Peter Hall took over). Two younger members of the ensemble - Patsy Byrne and Roy Dotrice - led the cast along with two more guests, Michael Flanders (of Flanders and Swan) as the narrator, and Hugh Griffith as Azdak. Leslie Caron (married to Peter Hall at that time) joined the company to play the title role in Giraudoux's *Ondine*, opposite Richard Johnson.

John Wyckham designed the lighting for most of the productions (he had also done the lighting for *Oliver*) and came with us for the first week when we took two of the plays on a national tour. That first week was spent in Edinburgh as part of the International Festival, an event to which I would return as often as possible over the next thirty years, both as participant and spectator. For the rest of the tour I was on my own, trying to reproduce John's lighting with whatever equipment was available in the different theatres. My first-ever tour, and I was already re-lighting major productions by the Royal Shakespeare Company: this was really learning on-the-job. Fortunately we had an excellent stage manager, David Brierley (who progressed very quickly to General Manager and remained with the company until his retirement in 1996), and everything went reasonably smoothly.

In 1963 Peter Hall was planning his extraordinary *Wars Of The Roses* season for Stratford-on-Avon, and had engaged John Bury to design the sets. The results, with metal walls and steel stage, became part of theatre history. John had learnt his craft coping with the exacting demands of Joan Littlewood for her Theatre Workshop company at Stratford East. He was one of the first to dispense with the footlights, and his realistic sets included concrete walls and the original 'kitchen sink'. John Bury eventually became Head of Design at the National Theatre, again teaming up with (by then) Sir Peter Hall, and later received Tony Awards for his designs and lighting for *Amadeus* on Broadway.

After years of struggle following their move south from Manchester, Theatre Workshop had just had an enormous success with *Oh What A Lovely War*. This was about to move into the West End, but John was fully occupied with the *Wars Of The Roses* and couldn't be released. In a football-style transfer deal I was part-exchanged, and reproduced John's lighting for the London opening at Wyndham's Theatre, and eventually for the British and German tours - yes, we actually toured *Oh What a Lovely War* in West Germany: they loved it. Sadly, John Bury was available for the New York production, so I missed out on my one real chance to work on Broadway.

However, I did have that opportunity to work with Joan Littlewood, one of the most energetic and original people in British theatre. *Oh What A Lovely War* was the undoubted peak of Joan Littlewood's career but its success in London and New York made stars of her actors. They moved on to other things and without her company of clowns (her word, not mine) much of the focus of her energy had dissipated. Her influence lives on in so many ways, and she was certainly a key part of my own personal learning curve.

Joan had a flat in Paris for many years, and we met up there occasionally: her enthusiasm never flagged, and dinner in her favourite little Greek restaurant was a rewarding experience. On one occasion she 'reprised' her meeting that same afternoon with two energetic and voluble American ladies, playing all three roles in an exhausting but brilliant *piece de theatre* which had me and the restaurant staff in stitches. She was always off somewhere, usually to be feted at some foreign festival or conference, and the last time we met she was working on a project to put the entire history of Australia on the stage. A wonderful, inspirational lady, whose talents and achievements have never been sufficiently acknowledged in her own country.

The Royal Shakespeare Company finally gave me the chance to combine theatre and travel when they sent me with the Peter Brook production of *King Lear* to the *Theatre des Nations* Festival in Paris. Paul Scofield was Lear, with Alec McCowen as his Fool and Irene Worth as Goneril. It was my very first trip to France, and my first experience of a 9.00pm curtain up. The performance didn't finish until after midnight when Marlene Dietrich climbed on to her seat to lead the standing ovation. I well remember how surprised, delighted and relieved we were to find the bars and cafes still open when we left the theatre. A few weeks later *Oh What A Lovely War* also appeared at the Festival des Nations and shared the judges award for best production - with *King Lear*.

Chapter Ten: From Angouleme to the National Theatre.

I'd been looking after the neighbours' pets while they visited the UK for half-term, and clearly not doing it very well because the guinea pig died. I told the builder who was working on their bedroom extension and he said "That's all guinea pigs do, isn't it. Eat, sleep, shit and die". The two young daughters were going to be upset when they returned, but that's a risk you take when you leave pets at the mercy of neighbours or relations. I remember two theatre colleagues who went off on tour leaving granny to look after their pets, and returned to find her on the doorstep, wringing her hands. "I'm never going to look after your animals again" she sobbed. "The dog got out and got run over, and the tropical fish have all boiled away".

The immediate problem was the rabbit, who had shared a run with the guinea pig and was looking lonely. We had a rabbit in a production of Cinderella in the old Byre Theatre in St Andrews. The rabbit was supposed to hop around the stage during the first scene when Cinderella is gathering sticks. She would pick it up and stroke it, and then propel it towards the wings where we caught it and returned it to its hutch. After a few performances it developed a strange rash which the vet diagnosed as stage fright. Fortunately we had an understudy which, in true showbiz fashion, took over at short notice and revelled in the role, being photographed by the press the following morning and achieving instant stardom.

I didn't want another stressed rabbit so I sought a replacement guinea pig, preferably one similar in size and colour to the dear-departed on the principle that you can fool some of the people some of the time. Any mother who has lost the school hamster during the holidays will understand the situation. This meant a trip, in the rain, to the big city - our county town of Angoulême. Founded by the Romans, it proved an impregnable fortress in medieval times but the ancient fortifications have since been 'topped' with boulevards, known as the *Remparts*, built over the old city walls and offering magnificent views in all directions.

19th century Town Hall incorporating parts of the original castle, and rubbish bins decorated with cartoon characters.

Today's Angoulême is a modern, bustling capital city with a population of around 50,000 and, at the end of January, home to *La Salon Internationale de la Bande Dessinée* - an enormous celebration of the art of the strip cartoon. The Salon takes over the entire city centre, the market hall, the theatres and galleries, and specially-erected marquees known as 'bubbles' (not the warmest of venues in January). Shopkeepers join in the fun by decorating their premises in the style of their favourite cartoon.

You might think that this is an unusual subject for a festival, but perhaps not in Angoulême where paper-making was (and still is) one of its principal industries. The first mill opened on the River Lizonne in 1516, and by 1656 there were no less than sixty-six paper-mills on the Charente and its tributaries, producing high quality watermarked paper that was exported via the river as far as Holland and London. Probably the best-known export is RIZLA+ cigarette papers, the name derived from *riz* (rice paper) and *La Croix* (the name of the founder).

Some mills had to close when their protestant workers fled the country in 1685. One of them, *Le Nil*, has re-opened as a Museum of Paper. Another, *Les Chais Magellis*, is now *La Musée de la Bande Dessinée,* and you can find them both just along the river from the Port l'Houmeau, or below the Market Hall if you can cope with the steps and the steep slopes. I got really lucky on this trip because the 2015 exhibition in *La Musée du Papier* introduced me to the fantastic - and for once the word is justified - works of French artist Bernard Pras. The notes tell me that "*he works almost entirely within the realm of assemblage and anamorposis, a visual illusion where a distorted projection - often made from paint, or a collection of objects - must be viewed from a specific vantage point to reconstitute the intended image*". No, I'm not sure that I entirely understood that either, but the works themselves are extraordinary. You move around what appears to be a three-dimensional display of rubbish until, from just one position, everything lines up to form an incredible work of art. Seek out his works, or check him out on the internet.

By comparison, I found *La Musée de la Bande Dessinée* a tiny bit sterile. Architecturally interesting, with a terrific and wide-ranging collection of exhibits, but my French wasn't strong enough to comprehend the themes and links - if indeed there were any themes and links. But do go there, if only to see the incredible building across the bridge, The International City of Comics and Image. The 'City' occupies a refurbished former brewery, and includes a museum, a media library, a digital imaging laboratory and the European School of Image. The building is a striking 'image' itself, designed by architect Jean Giraud who works under the *nom-de-plume* Moebius. In 2012 the structure was officially renamed, in his honour, *Le Vaisseau Moebius* - The Moebius Spaceship.

Bernard Pras - and The Spaceship.

In Angoulême, paper was originally produced by hand, sheet by sheet, and the industry only became mechanised in the 19th century. The skilled mechanics developing that trade would later become involved locally in the development of the motor car. The motoring connection continues as Angouleme still has one of the only three street-races in France, the *Circuit des Remparts*, re-enacted on the middle Sunday in September and usually involving some ancient Bugattis. Since the *Remparts* are barely wide enough for two lanes of regular traffic one wonders just how much overtaking is practical during these races.

To the north of the city a monument marks the site where Marcel Renault, winner of the Paris-Vienna race in 1902, died in an accident while competing in the 1903 Paris-Madrid race. Excessive speeds (one car was clocked at a terrifying 74mph) coupled with deaths and injuries to drivers and spectators caused the French and Spanish governments to put an end to the race.

A former paper mill at Ruelle was bought by the Marquis de Montalembert in 1750 and developed as a foundry for the manufacture of naval cannons. Ruelle was close to mineral deposits, to timber from the forest of Braconne, and to water from the River Touvre which provided a steady flow for the mill as well as access to the Charente for the transport of 800 cannon to the naval arsenal at Rochefort, 100 kilometres downstream. Eventually there would be a railway line from the foundry to the Port de l'Houmeau on the Angouleme quayside, where a crane was built to load the cannon onto boats. A regular cargo for these boats on their return trips from the coast was salt, and the Port de l'Houmeau had been developed at the head of the navigable part of the river to handle this trade. From the port the salt was distributed to the hinterland by cart, leading to the development of other crafts in the area - notably wheelwrights and saddlers - as well as the construction of better housing for the merchants profiting from the trade. Today, the Port de l'Houmeau is busy again, not with cargo boats but with pleasure craft.

Because of its geographical position Angoulême has often found itself piggy-in-the-middle between opposing forces: indeed, it is said that during the 300 Years War (1153-1453) the occupants changed their 'passports' a thousand times. Naturally, the English were involved. It all started when Eleanor of Aquitaine married Henry II in 1152, incorporating the area from Charente down to Bordeaux into Henry's 'Angevin Empire'. In 1264 Isabelle, the daughter of Guillaume Taillefer (*Cut-Iron*? remember him?) was defeated by Louis IX at Taillebourg, and Angoulême was French again. I hope you're making notes: we'll be visiting Taillebourg later in the book, and some of this might be important.

The struggles went on: the 1360 Treaty of Bretigny put the English back in charge, and the Prince of Wales moved his headquarters into Angoulême Castle. Twelve years later the French, under Charles V, were back, but couldn't prevent English incursions from pillaging and ruining the city. Eventually, Charles VII's victory at Castillon cleared the English out of Aquitaine. The region was exhausted and depopulated: settlers came from Poitou to help with the regeneration. Nowadays the settlers come from Britain, buying retirement homes or *maisons secondaires*. Some believe it to be official British policy to buy back Aquitaine 'house by house; farm by farm'.

The arrivals in September 1939 were refugees from the north; as many as 18,000 in a single day, all needing food, lodging and work. When the Nazis arrived the traffic was in the opposite direction: on 8th October 1942 they rounded up 325 Jews and transported them to Auschwitz in animal trucks. The next year more than 3,500 young men were sent off to work as slave labour in German factories. The Resistance was active, but so was the Gestapo: 249 civilians were shot, and hundreds more deported. The Allies bombed the station at Angoulême to stop the Germans using the railway line.

140 civilians were killed and more than 100 injured in the raids, but the line was back in use after three days. The resistance was heroic and Angoulême has a Museum devoted to 'The Resistance and the Deportation' in *la rue de Genève*. Sadly, there was a downside - treatment of collaborators, even suspected collaborators, was sometimes as brutal as anything dished out by the Gestapo.

On a lighter note, a local joke. "All Charente towns have a name ending in -*ac*. For example, Angoulême, Barbezieux, Chateauneuf, La Rochefoucauld......". Alright, I didn't say it was a funny joke (perhaps it's one of Peter Hall's), but the mention of La Rochefoucauld reminds me of an invention by Mr Gay, a cobbler in that town at the end of the 17th century. One day he found himself with off-cuts of the naval greatcoats manufactured in La Rochefoucauld, and also with pieces of felt, a by-product of the paper industry. He put them together and, *voila*, a carpet slipper - known to this day as a Charentaise. By the nineteen-thirties there were 60 slipper-makers, sewing by hand or with rudimentary machines, and experimenting with soles in leather or rubber, even bits of car tyres. By the nineteen-eighties the firm of Rondinaud, who had first sold slippers in their shop in 1847, was producing five million pairs a year. That's a lot of chopped-up greatcoats.... 'My Slipper And Me' was the title chosen by James Rondinaud for his life story.

In my own life story, one of the most significant events was a phone call. "Sir Laurence Olivier wants to see you", I was told. "You're to meet him tomorrow afternoon at Chichester". Sir Laurence (later Lord) Olivier, the outstanding actor of his generation and something of a god to those of us in the lower ranks of the profession, had been the obvious choice to head Britain's first National Theatre Company. They had opened in the renovated Old Vic Theatre in 1962, and were spending the 1963 summer season performing on the thrust stage at Chichester's Festival Theatre.

Sir Laurence appeared at the stage door in shirtsleeves and suggested that we went for a chat, which we did, sitting on the lawns at the back of the theatre. The National operated the 'repertoire' system, with a different play every evening, and two different plays on matinee days. He explained that during his first season he had used guest designers for both scenery and lighting. Naturally enough they had all wanted to make a good impression and had made such full use of the equipment (and budgets) available that the theatre staff were finding it difficult to change the scenery, and to re-focus and re-colour practically every spotlight in the building in the limited time available at the end of each day's rehearsals.

"What I want you to do" he said, "is to join us as resident lighting designer, and plan a basic lighting rig which will adapt quickly to the different productions". Inexperienced as I was, I knew this was an impossible dream but that didn't stop me accepting his offer. I felt that I had arrived. After only a few years in the profession I had been personally invited by Olivier to join his National Theatre Company. I phoned my parents with the news. Dad's reaction was entirely predictable: "Isn't it time you gave all this up and got a proper job?" But they didn't return their tickets for my first night.

I should perhaps explain, as briefly as possible, why a basic lighting rig for a repertoire theatre is an impossible dream (anyone who's eyes glaze over when a technician - usually with his back to a bar counter - starts to detail the intricacies of his profession should probably skip the next couple of paragraphs).

The National Theatre's second Old Vic season would open with a mixture of revivals from the first year and the transfer from Chichester of *The Royal Hunt Of The Sun*. These productions were already in existence: I could work with the models of the set designs, check the colours of costumes, talk to the directors. Two further productions were already announced, and I would have early indication of their requirements, but the final productions of that season were still undecided. My brief was to design a lighting rig that would adapt to shows that had not yet been selected, and to sets and costumes which had not yet been designed. They might be open stage productions like *Othello* or *Mother Courage*; they might fill the stage with happy scenery like *Hay Fever* or *Hobson's Choice*: I simply did not know. And with many of the earlier productions remaining in the repertoire there would be limited opportunities to adjust the rig mid-season.

So why was I offered this poisoned chalice? To some extent it was a shrewd choice: I had spent two years with the Royal Shakespeare Company at the Aldwych Theatre (where they also operated the repertoire system) working alongside their Lighting Designer, John Wyckham, so I had relevant experience and understood the problems. Indeed, plenty of people understood the problems, which were common to the Royal Opera House, the RSC, and every opera and ballet company presenting a repertoire of productions using different designers. The restrictions of time and space - and budgets - at the Old Vic were forcing Sir Laurence to seek a solution, but reining in the lighting potential while still giving free rein to the directors and set designers was certain to lead to an imbalance which would become more noticeable as the season progressed.

Knowing all this, why did I accept the challenge? Silly question: I was never going to turn down the chance to spend a year at the National, with Olivier and Franco Zeffirelli and Noel Coward and the cream of British acting talent. Of course, it would only be for a year: the system would limit the artistic lighting possibilities, and the experiment would not be repeated. More importantly, I already knew that I did not want to continue as a lighting designer: I had got into it by accident, but would get out by choice - I had other plans.

Better, therefore, that I take the blame rather than a dedicated young lighting specialist - and there were several talented guys around, some of them already on the Old Vic staff, who would be free to do their own thing once the idea of a 'permanent rig' was dismissed as 'unworkable'.

photo by Chris Arthur: lighting by Brian Freeland.

Despite these misgivings, it was a great year while it lasted: *Royal Hunt of the Sun* arrived from its summer season at Chichester starring Robert Stephens and Colin Blakely. Olivier took over the role of Solness in *The Master Builder* and revived his acclaimed *Othello,* and his strong company included Maggie Smith, Frank Finlay, Derek Jacobi, Celia Johnson, Lynn Redgrave, Anthony Nicholls, Joyce Redman, Michael Gambon, Robert Lang and Max Adrian. The pace was horrendous - we opened a new production every three weeks, and changed the shows in repertoire every night.

Olivier had two associate directors: John Dexter had directed *Othello* and *Royal Hunt Of The Sun*, and would later move to New York as Director of the Metropolitan Opera. Bill Gaskill directed *The Dutch Courtesan*, *The Recruiting Officer*, and *Mother Courage*, and would take over the Royal Court Theatre following George Devine's retirement. Olivier himself directed the final production of the season, Arthur Miller's *The Crucible*, with the author present at the first night. We also had a couple of guest directors.

The company was running along smoothly churning out yet another classic every few weeks until the exuberant Italian, Franco Zeffirelli, arrived to shake us all up with a madcap production of *Much Ado About Nothing* played, at Olivier's suggestion, in cod Italian accents. Zeffirelli had studied to be an architect and, like his great mentor Luchino Visconti, preferred to design as well as direct. His brightly coloured sets and costumes for *Much Ado* were inspired by the Jewish folk art paintings of Mark Chagall.

According to Picasso, "when Matisse dies, Chagall will be the only painter left who understands what colour really is". Robert Stephens and Maggie Smith were superb as the lovers (a role they continued offstage); Albert Finney joined the company to play Don Pedro; and Frank Finlay was a very funny, bike-riding Dogberry. Nino Rota (the composer who won an Oscar for Godfather Part Two) was commissioned to write some 'village band' music which absolutely caught the mood of the production: and was recorded on an EP disc but there is no copy in the NT Archives. No 'record' of a National Theatre commission from one of the leading 20th century composers. However, I discovered recently that Nino had probably recycled some material from two of his earlier films *Il Bidone* (1955) and *Plein Soleil/Purple Noon* (1960), so perhaps the loss is not as significant as I feared.

Two weeks before the opening Zeffirelli turned up with designs for a huge arch to go at the front of the stage, a metal framework with thousands of miniature light bulbs wired into three circuits - a different colour and a different pattern for each circuit. When told that it wasn't possible in the time (or in the budget) he shrugged his shoulders and said "so, I go back to Italy". It was made, of course: a nightmare for the technicians, but providing a beautifully coloured frame for each of the two acts and the finale of this joyous production.

Dame Edith Evans joined us to play Judith Bliss in Noel Coward's *Hay Fever* directed by the author himself. The great lady was by then in her late seventies, still with tremendous ability and star quality but nervous about playing someone twenty years younger, and not at all confident about her lines. We did a week in Manchester before opening at the Old Vic, and she locked herself in her hotel room unable to face the dress rehearsal. Noel had to go and reassure her, and told us later "I found myself picking her up and saying Edith, I'm only doing this because I love you, and all the time all I wanted to do was shove my fist very hard right up her fanny". There was one small hiatus on the first night when she 'dried', she forgot her lines. The stage manager offered a prompt which was heard by the front row but not by Dame Edith. The second was audible in the circle, but she still didn't catch it. After the third prompt had echoed round the theatre she turned to Anthony Nicholls, playing her husband, and enquired "What did he say?".

You could feel the nervous tension on stage, and in the auditorium. Happily, a few moments later, she pitched one of Coward's wittier lines absolutely perfectly and got a huge laugh. This relaxed the tension and the evening ended as a great success.

Noel Coward was a 'tax exile' at that time, only allowed to work in Britain for 90 days a year, so he fitted as much as he could into the 90 days. During the rehearsals for *Hay Fever* he compered and introduced *A Night at the Theatre*, a televised evening of excerpts from some of the best shows in the West End recorded at one of H M Tennant's venues (I can't remember which). I was vaguely involved because one of the excerpts was from the National Theatre production of *The Master Builder* with Olivier as Solness and Maggie Smith as Hilde, although it was Tennant's lighting man Joe Davis (no, not the snooker-playing Joe Davis) who was helping the TV crew with the lighting. During the afternoon run-through I noticed that Coward was aiming all his introductions to the Stalls, but being filmed from the Circle: all you could see on the monitor screen was the top of his head. One hesitates to give notes to The Master but I did mention this to him in the tea-break, and the Dress Circle certainly got the full benefit of his wit and wisdom throughout the evening's performance.

Before *Hay Fever* opened, I was watching a rehearsal from the back of the circle. Celia Johnson came and sat beside me, watching Dame Edith on stage, and suddenly whispered "Oh, I do wish they would let me understudy her". Of course the whole idea was preposterous: a star of Celia's experience under-studying anyone, even Dame Edith, but during a break in rehearsals I passed on her thoughts to Mr Coward. Celia not only covered for Dame Edith, but took over the role later in the run - and was perfect. She once said, at another star's crowded memorial service, "there won't be so many when I go: you'll have to paper the house". Eventually, when that sad day came, I was at her memorial service, and it was standing room only. Conversation with Celia was occasionally rather surreal: she had wonderful throw-away lines such as "we had some friends round for tea: The Queen Mother and one or two others".

I have always regretted that by the time I discovered the theatre it was just too late to catch that particular generation of stars at their best. Too late to enjoy Dame Edith as Rosalind or Millament or Lady Bracknell, for instance, or Sir John Gielgud as Hamlet, or Sir Ralph Richardson's Falstaff. It was wonderful to watch Dame Peggy Ashcroft every night in *The Duchess Of Malfi* and *The Cherry Orchard*, but I never had the thrill of seeing her in Shakespeare. I saw Dame Sybil Thorndike as *Saint Teresa of Avila* but never as *St Joan*. Even at the Palladium I missed the great days of the Music Hall although I did just catch Randolph Sutton, George Formby, Ida Barr and Hetty King in live performances right at the end of their careers. Not at the height of their powers, but one was still aware of the quality.

Similarly with Dame Edith in *Hay Fever*. Even in a *souflet* of a part such as Judith Bliss there was still the glamour, the timing, the humour, the unique abilities that mark genuine star quality. I heard her reading (beautifully, and with great warmth and humour) some poetry on the BBC in that incredible voice of hers. Everybody has heard impressions of Dame Edith as Lady Bracknell with that highly individual vocalisation of "A handbag?", but not everyone realises that she spoke like that pretty much all the time. Nevertheless, it was alleged that, during rehearsals for a new play, *Gentle Jacks*, she asked the producers "Do we have to have that Kenneth Williams in the company? He's got the most peculiar voice". I suspect that she was actually quite a lonely person. Kenneth Williams wrote that she complained to him after a performance of *Gentle Jacks*, "None of the actors come along to my room for a chat". When he hinted "Well, you're a cult, they view you with awe" she responded "No, I'm very ordinary really. I sit at home on my little stool with my apron on and I baste the joint with my old wooden spoon. Oh yes, I am very ordinary, very roast beef and yorkshire pudding".

Olivier was always treated with awe and, like Dame Edith, didn't always enjoy it. I remember him rushing into the office one day clutching the hat from his costume and yelling "Why didn't you bastards tell me how awful this thing looked. I've never liked it, but everyone is always so deferential - afraid to say anything that might upset me". People used to say of Olivier that the lights appeared to brighten when he walked onto a stage, and they were very often right: the electricians had been instructed to do exactly that. He told me that he didn't want anything special for his first entrance as *Othello*, but I plotted a little something with the director, John Dexter, and if 'Sir' noticed it he didn't complain. *Othello* wasn't an easy show to light. Olivier was using a very black make-up and wearing a dark-coloured costume, while Maggie Smith as Desdemona was all in white. I used a lot of blue light, which seemed to reflect better from the black face but toned down Desdemona's whiteness, and noticed that director Stuart Burge did the same for his 1965 film.

I was not too sorry when my year ended. I found it most frustrating not being able to treat each production as a one-off, and I have never enjoyed repertoire. Every night becomes a first night: you never get a run of two or three shows where you can work on the 'fine tuning'. Besides, I was still learning my trade. It was time to hit the road, move on, learn something else.

Bill Gaskill was about to take over from George Devine as Director at the Royal Court and asked me to join him. "Why?" I asked: "we're always arguing". "That's exactly why", he said. "You always question me, make me think about what I'm doing". "Join you in what role? (*please, please, please say associate director)"*. "I'll need a lighting designer". He got one - Andy Phillips, whose talents were ideally suited to the Royal Court style of production, and he did some excellent work there.

I said thank you and goodbye to Sir Laurence. He thought I was off to Bayreuth to stage manage Wagner opera and, still in awe, I didn't correct him. In fact, I was off to Beirut, to stage manage topless cabaret in a huge casino. And some more on-the-job experience.

Chapter Eleven: From Paris to Beirut to Paris.

It was in the theatre bar at Sadlers Wells one evening that the wife of the theatre manager asked if I would be interested in working in the Middle East. She needed a stage manager for a massive Las Vegas-style production in the *Casino du Liban* in Beirut. My year at the National was nearly finished and I had nothing lined up so - naturally - I said "yes".

The polyglot company - British, French and American - was gathering in Paris for rehearsals, and it was there that I met the production team for the first time. Ron Fields, the experienced American choreographer, was already hard at work with the usual night club mix of stately, top-heavy showgirls and lithe, athletic dancers. Producer/director of this extravaganza was a short, stout, pompously aggressive Russian emigré named Charley Henchis. If he had any talent at all, which I dispute, it was in the field of larceny since every idea in his overblown production had been stolen from Broadway, Las Vegas and the West End.

Horses galloping on treadmills through clouds of dry ice; a train full of visitors arriving at a station; a Spanish *Corrida*; a mobile ice rink; a topless swimmer inside a giant hubble-bubble bottle. All stolen. All shoe-horned clumsily into his 'production' with very little sense of artistic integrity. As the Spectator wrote of a later Henchis spectacular *"It is all a bit threadbare in cultural values"*.

This pocket-sized Mr Big was having trouble finding a lighting designer and questioned me about the British specialists, in particular Michael Northern, chairman of the Society of Lighting Designers. Michael could have written the book on artistic integrity and would have hated everything about this Charley Henchis set-up so I suggested some other names. He eventually contracted Tharon Musser (not one of my suggestions), the most prolific - and talented - lighting designer in American theatre history who later specialised in lighting Broadway musicals for the likes of Stephen Sondheim, Jerry Herman and Michael Bennett.

Eventually it was time to decamp to Beirut. We had an early flight and, forgetting that we had Americans in the company, I told them I had arranged for them all to be knocked up at five the following morning.

At the airport Little Big Man handed me a large glass balloon filled with a dark liquid: he wanted smoke effects for his production and he had been working with Paris chemists to produce this liquid which, on contact with the air, immediately filled any space (room, stage, aeroplane?) with thick, slightly smelly vapour. "Keep hold of that until we land" he said. I would rather have held a bomb, but to argue with Charley - sorry, to argue with Mr Henchis - was to risk immediate dismissal and I desperately wanted to see Beirut. Somehow I got the bottle through Customs, but it was a nightmare journey. I didn't even dare go to the toilet - and boy, how I wanted to.

The Casino du Liban first opened in 1959. The Cabaret Room had been destroyed by fire in the mid-sixties and was supposed to be rebuilt and ready in time for our arrival. Unsurprisingly, it wasn't, and we continued rehearsals for several weeks in the fully-equipped theatre which formed another part of the Casino complex. The Casino held the sole concession for gaming in the Lebanon, and was a huge magnet attracting gamblers from all over the Middle East. Mainly Arab Muslim gamblers; all in formal dinner suits with black tie. The Complex was privately owned, but the State took 65% of gross gaming revenue which, to re-assure Muslim susceptibilities, had to be used for 'good works'. Good works as defined by the Ministry of Social Affairs, so it was never clear at that time where the money actually went. The nightclub floor show, with its topless showgirls and leggy dancers, brought in even more punters, and the Casino was said to be an even bigger earner for the State than the Roman Temple at Baalbeck.

We were eventually allowed to move into the Cabaret Room where Charley - sorry, Mr Henchis - was to stage what The Spectator called *his showgirl-infested spectacle*. We started with night-time fit-ups and rehearsals while the builders completed their tasks during the day. Then, as opening night drew ever closer, we began to run sections of the show with costumes and props. Our Musical Director, a Frenchman by the name of Eddie Guerin, had been in the orchestra pit on the night of the fire which destroyed the old Cabaret Room and had clearly not forgotten the experience. The rebuilt Night Club had his band on top of a mushroom-shaped tower just by the stage right proscenium, and he was taking them through the rehearsal of a big production number involving, amongst other things, a juggler and fire-eater who was using his props on stage for the first time. Eddie looked up from his music, saw the flames being thrown around on stage, and was down the stairs and out into the car park in less than ten seconds flat. Didn't even stop to pick up his music scores.

Tharon Musser was much too busy and talented a lady to sit around in Beirut waiting for the builders to finish. She'd returned to New York and sent one of her assistants out to Beirut. He did a good job on the lighting - the Spanish routines in the Corrida set were particularly atmospheric - but it was all much too artistic for Charley - sorry, Mr Henchis. Before the second performance he had the staff remove all coloured filters from the spotlights, and pushed all the dimmers to full. He knew how I felt about this kind of thing: discussions were acrimonious and, inevitably, I was 'allowed to go'. A Lebanese manager immediately offered me a job in a smaller cabaret room in the centre of Beirut, but Mr Henchis - sorry, little Charley - refused to transfer my work permit and I had to return to London. I did go back to Beirut after the six-day war - but more of that in a later chapter.

My appreciation of French culture had started long before my sojourn in that country. There were the films, of course, at the school cinema club and at the Tatler in Bristol, and I had started to develop an interest in the French impressionist painters, but I think the first French theatre production that I ever saw was a revue, *La Plume de Ma Tante*, written by and starring Robert Dhéry with his wife Collette Brosset.

L to R: Colette Brosset, Pierre Olaf, Christian Duvaleix, Robert Dhéry and Jacques Legras, the stars of the show.

The format was not unlike a Crazy Gang show: in fact, the Crazy Gang had used one of his sketches, Frère Jacques, a routine for innocent monks having a bit of fun swinging on the bell-ropes. Another item in *La Plume de Ma Tante* had Miss Brosset joining the dancers for a black light routine set in the jungle, and then suddenly producing a torch so that she could see where she was going and not bump into the other dancers. "It's crazy" she would mutter, "dancing in the dark; it's so dangerous". Good visual humour. George Devine, a man I never met but greatly admired and who was largely responsible for the successful revival of the Royal Court Theatre in the nineteen-fifties, saw what he called "Robert Dhéry's masterpiece of organised disaster" and wistfully told a friend "I've wanted to do that all my life".

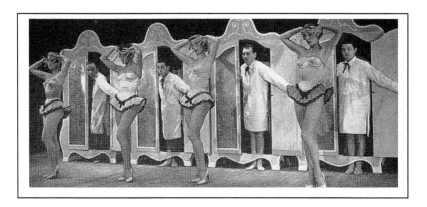

The French are natural actors. They act all of the time. Watch two people talking in the street; the arms never stop gesticulating, the eyes are alive and forever reacting to whatever the other person is saying whether they are discussing the fall of the government or the price of plums. Their theatre is similarly physical (unlike their television where people never stop talking, usually into enormous hand-held microphones). While British actors are undoubtedly world champions in the use of the voice, the continentals can teach us a great deal about acting with the entire body.

And not just the continentals: I remember laughing out loud at a sort of Will Hay sketch performed in Gujarati in Bombay, and enjoying a rehearsal of *The Government Inspector* in Addis Ababa without understanding a single word of either. The body language was enough.

The intriguing black light puppet shows of Philipe Gentry, and the enchanting *Le Cirque Imaginaire* of Victoria Chaplin and her husband John-Baptiste Thierrée have delighted audiences throughout the world, even those who speak not a word of French. It probably helped that Victoria was the daughter of Charles (and Oona) Chaplin, and the grand-daughter of Eugene O'Neill.

Two of my outstanding memories of French theatre are both visual. The first was in *Les Petits Pas*, a charming little play that Frank Dunlop brought to the Edinburgh Festival. It had a running gag (I'm a sucker for running gags) involving a lady throwing an empty wine bottle into a bin at the back of the set every time she crossed the stage. On the last throw the bin, together with the entire back wall, completely and suddenly disappeared, leaving an enormous hole. The play ended with the cast all slowly returning to peer into this hole, silhouetted against a whiff of white smoke rising from below.

On one of my irregular visits to Paris I saw Dario Fo's production of Molière's *Le Bourgois Gentilhomme* for the Comédie Francaise. The prologue had a large tree centre stage, with an actor slowly sawing through the branch on which he was sitting. We all sat spellbound, waiting for the seemingly-inevitable crash but knowing that there had to be a gag in it somewhere - after all, you don't normally kill off (perhaps literally) an important character in the first few minutes. Sure enough, as he made the final cut, it was the tree which crashed to the ground, leaving the actor suspended in mid-air still sitting happily on his branch.

Some French productions are memorable for all the wrong reasons. I was a guest of the Paris branch of the International Theatre Institute for the first night of a production of *Die Fledermaus* at the Paris Opera House which was so bizarre - with bare-buttocked dancers, and lighting which shone directly into our faces - that the audience complained loudly throughout the performance, and roundly booed the director when he bravely (if foolishly) took a bow at the end.

Chapter Twelve: From Berlin to Sri Lanka.

My National Service in Hong Kong had given me the taste for foreign travel, and I have been fortunate that my theatrical work has allowed me to indulge that appetite. For instance, a three-week holiday from my RSC stint at the Aldwych was spent hitch-hiking around Germany visiting their theatres, many of which had been rebuilt after the war and were equipped with all the latest technology. I had been warned that the buildings were impressive, so large that you needed a car to drive from one side of the stage to the other, and began to believe it when I arrived at Cologne Opera House to see an Austin Mini being driven out of the scenery dock doors.

Although I usually arrived unannounced, I was made welcome everywhere except the East Berlin Opera House: *"We're closed; come back next month*!" Sometimes I was even offered overnight accommodation by the theatre technicians. The highlight was a trip through the Berlin Wall to visit the Theater am Schiffbauerdamm, home of Brecht's Berliner Ensemble, where I was invited to watch a rehearsal of *The Good Woman of Setzuan* - still rehearsing although it had been in the repertoire for nearly three years - and had the pleasure of meeting his widow Helene Weigel. I noticed that they had a display of books about Brecht in the foyer, and was delighted to donate the copy of Eric Bentley's biography which had been part of my reading material on the trip.

My first full-scale overseas tour was to the Indian sub-continent during the winter of 1962/63. We left London on Boxing Day only a few hours before blizzards closed not just Heathrow but most of the country, the start of one of the worst winters ever in Britain although we only heard about it in letters and newspaper cuttings arriving from home. The company was the Bristol Old Vic led by that same Denis Carey who had directed Peter O'Toole in Man And Superman during the early days of my National Service, and we took a repertoire of three plays - *Hamlet, Arms And The Man*, and *A Man For All Seasons*. A fine actor (later teacher, and Director of RADA) Oliver Neville, played Sir Thomas More and Claudius, and directed *Arms And The Man*. Denis Carey, whose recent production of *Salad Days* was proving such a hit in the West End, directed the other two. A tireless Liz Charnley was the stage manager, and I was looking after lighting and scenery. We saw in the 1963 New Year during a dress rehearsal of *Hamlet* in Karachi.

The tour was under the auspices of the British Council, and took us through West and East Pakistan (now Pakistan and Bangladesh), India and Ceylon (now Sri Lanka). In Dacca we performed in the Railway Institute, and stayed in a ramshackle hotel where, if you needed hot water for a wash or shave, you shouted over the balcony and the bearers put some buckets on an open fire in the courtyard below. Staying in that same hotel was guitarist Julian Bream, also on a British Council tour but going in the opposite direction. He joined us for dinner in the hotel restaurant where they had an elderly quartet playing songs from the shows during the meal. Julian enlivened the proceedings by leaping up on the stage with his guitar and announcing that "the boys and I are going to swing some Cole Porter", which they did. Wonderfully.

From there we went into India playing mostly in older venues such as the New Empire Theatre in Calcutta. This had been an opera house until the late fifties, when cinema projection equipment was installed, and it is now only used for films. Calcutta also had a Garrison Theatre during (and after) the war, the hall of St Xavier's College, headquarters for the ENSA shows touring under the management of actor Jack Hawkins. We stayed at the Grand Hotel, living in imperial splendour by comparison with the poverty on the streets outside. The hotel was on Chowringhee, opposite the Maidan, just a few streets away from the enormous covered market where we learned that it was easier to pay a basket-carrying porter a few annas to accompany you through the souk, even if you had nothing to carry, than to fight off the hordes of prospective 'guides'. It was harder to resist the outstretched hands of the numerous child beggars. On a later tour the actors in the company refused to engage a rickshaw because, they said, it was immoral to expect another human being to drag you around the streets, and did I know that the life expectation of a rickshaw man was only about thirty-five years? I pointed out that it was his job: he rented the rickshaw and if he didn't get any customers then he couldn't pay the rent for his rickshaw or his home, and his family might not eat that evening. There was a great discussion in the dressing room throughout the show but by curtain down they had solved the moral dilemma: they hired rickshaws, which they then pulled back to the hotel themselves with the amused, if slightly embarrassed, rickshaw-wallahs riding in the back.

I have toured India eight times with different companies and the memories are all confused: theatres, hotels, airports, cities and people all coalesce into a giant, colourful, kaleidoscopic memory. Indeed, I have already jumbled two quite separate tours in the previous paragraphs. We did all the obvious, touristy things like visiting the Taj Mahal, which really is stunning - and quite theatrical in a way because you don't enter through the 'front door' but along a narrow dark corridor until you suddenly find yourself under that great arch looking down the line of ornamental pools and gardens towards that glorious white marble temple gleaming in the sunshine.

On Elephanta Island off Bombay we climbed the thousand steps to the Temple with the huge phallic statues; we took thrilling train rides up the mountains from Bombay to Poona, and from Colombo to Kandy, with the railway track hugging the edge - thick greenery to one side and a 400-foot drop to the other. On one tour we actually stayed in the Poona Club, the restaurant tables sparkling with white linen, crystal glasses and gleaming cutlery. The waiters looked splendid with their scarlet turbans and sashes - and only four of us dining. At another meal, the Deputy High Commissioner's wife fed us sausages and mash and baked beans which had been flown in especially from London because, as she explained, "I thought you might be getting a bit bored with chicken curry".

I remember animals: the three-legged dog in a little settlement behind our theatre in Mauritius which was universally ignored by villagers and dogs alike, but whose life was totally changed for four days when a bus-load of English actors moved into the theatre. Another group of English actors made a fuss over an animal in the Music Academy in Madras - only this animal was a monkey which had found its way up into the roof girders above the stage, and sat there piddling down on them throughout the performance.

The non-political status of the British Council meant that many National Leaders who might avoid High Commission events organised by their former Colonial masters, were happy to be seen at our touring productions. On that first Bristol Old Vic tour, Pandit Nehru attended Hamlet in New Delhi. On later tours we welcomed Mrs Ghandi. Mrs Banderaniake, The President of China and the Crown Prince of Nepal. In Karachi, the Pakistani President, General Ayub Khan, was in the front row of the circle and there were armed guards inside and outside the hall. I had been given strict instructions that, to ensure the President's safety, there should be no blackouts during the production. With our simple setting we needed the blackouts to get people on and off, and set furniture, so on the first scene change I disobeyed instructions and went to blackout. It was probably only five or six seconds before the lights came up again, but a very tense six seconds. I fully expected to find myself surrounded by angry soldiers pointing rifles, but nothing happened. No rifles; no soldiers marching me off to the cells; no dead President - so we just carried on and did the rest of the show as planned, with all of the black-outs.

Of all the National Leaders, I have happiest memories of the Emir of Kano, in Northern Nigeria. He came to a performance, clearly enjoyed himself, turned up at the British Council reception afterwards (he had been invited, but the Representative's house staff did not expect him to come) and as he left he invited us all to an audience at his Palace the following morning. 'Palace' sounds a bit grand for what was basically a single-storey mud-and-wattle building with battlements, but inside it was impressive. We were ushered into the Audience Chamber, a huge ornate throne at one end and a long row of chairs down each side, where we sat waiting. He entered in full Emiri Court dress, all gold cloth, including sash and turban, and those sandals with the curled-up toes which I'd only previously seen in pantomime, in Aladdin. We sat in audience for about twenty minutes asking about his country and his place in it, and then he said "Wait a minute while I get out of these things, and we'll go and have a drink". A Moslem Emir, remember, but he did enjoy a gin-and-tonic - and, I suspect, a wee touch of the 'theatrical'.

Kano is where they recently bombed the churches, but we were treated very well there - better, certainly, than in the supposedly Christian city of Lagos. Our Lagos performances were in the University Hall, and we turned up one evening to find that the sets and seating had been removed, and the hall used for a wedding party. A fairly riotous wedding party since all the tables and chairs were overturned; food, drink, broken crockery and glass littered the floor. The actors and the British Council staff cleared the hall and put the seats out, while I replaced the scenery and lighting. The show must go on and - in true British theatrical tradition - it did.

  Bigger companies such as the Bristol Old Vic normally only performed in the major cities - New Delhi, Bombay, Calcutta, Madras, and sometimes Bangalore: it was in Madras that we first made the acquaintance of perhaps the most remarkable man I have ever met.

David Horsburgh had been a Professor of English in Mysore before joining the British Council, and he arrived for the show with his 'understanding' wife Doreen in a beautifully-restored Austin Seven, one of several that he had shipped out (or driven out) from Britain. He had a passion for education, but not the 'lines of desks in front of a blackboard' type of education. He dreamt of a school which pupils attended because they wanted to and not because they 'jolly well had to'. A school with no rules, no failures, and no punishments. In 1972 he suddenly left the Council and opened his own school, Neel Bagh, in a rural village. He built the classroom himself, an Indian-style hut with a smooth highly-polished floor of beaten cow dung, and started with just two students, both boys from the local village. More village children soon enrolled, boys and girls, aged from five to fifteen. No exams, no classes, no grades. There was a timetable, but with the whole school working together on each subject, albeit at different levels and speeds. Like a family or village, David explained, with the younger ones absorbing the knowledge and experience of the older students."The thing to do is to get children to learn" he said.

"The more they learn the more they will want to learn. At Neel Bagh, if a child is bright he or she might get through four year's work in a single year, while a slower one might need eighteen months for one year's work, but both will be 'successful' at their own level". The system later became known as *Vikasana*, meaning blossoming, opening up, spreading - and the children responded enthusiastically to David's policy of development, the development of the individual, the group and the larger society.

He taught English to a standard that allowed his students to perform Shakespeare, not just in the school theatre (built by you-know-who) but, by invitation, in Bangalore and far-away Madras. When, I visited Neel Bagh, on what I guessed would be my final visit to India, some thirteen-year-olds were taking part in their seventh such Shakespeare production. They also studied the village language, Telegu; the state language, Kannada, and the national language, Hindi. Other subjects included Maths, Science, Environmental Studies, Arts and Crafts, Pottery and Carpentry, Philosophy, Musical Appreciation and Discussion Techniques. David financed all this by writing books for Oxford University Press.

His energy and enthusiasm were enormous - and infectious. With his long straggling hair he might have passed for a sadhu, a holy man, but he was like an uncle or a second father to his pupils. To me, he was as near to a saint as I am ever likely to meet. I was thrilled to visit Neel Bag, and privileged to attend his memorial service in 1984 when that great heart finally stopped beating. I am no longer a religious man - too many dreadful things are done every day in the name of religion - but I'm sure that if heaven exists then David will be there. Probably directing the angels in a production of *Loves Labours Lost*, in impeccable English of course, and showing them how to do proper stage lighting even without mains electricity. And financing it all by writing books for Paradise University Press.

Looking back, I suppose that my least-enjoyable Indian tour was with Prospect Productions. The British Council invited them to tour two plays, one classic and one contemporary. The modern play was quickly decided: Harold Pinter's *The Birthday Party*, but the classic proved more difficult. Shaw was the chosen author, but which play? The Council splits India into four administrative areas, at that time centred on Delhi, Calcutta, Madras and Bombay. The first three of these rarely offered any opposition to our play selections, but the Bombay office discussed every decision with the local theatre community, and in Bombay that was a huge - and extremely knowledgeable - community. There were probably more theatres operating in Bombay than in London's West End, and presenting shows in Marathi, Gujarati, Hindi and English. The longest run was perhaps three weeks (no long-running musicals such as *Cats* or *Les Miserables* in Bombay, and certainly no *Mousetrap*) so the turnover of productions was extravagant. Whichever Shaw play we offered them had been done, in one language or another, by one or other of the dozens of local companies. We went through all the more popular plays (and, more importantly, the plays which would double-cast with *The Birthday Party*): all were turned down by the Bombay office. Eventually, Bombay accepted *Misalliance* - an interesting, if wordy, play, with a cast of nine: *The Birthday Party* has a cast of six - so we would have three performers who would only be performing in one of the two plays. Then Equity, the actor's union, insisted that we carry understudies in case of injury or illness: one male and one female. So now we had three artistes in only one play, and two more who might possibly never appear in anything at all. Leading both casts were the talented and experienced Mona Washbourne and her husband Basil Dignam. I discovered only recently that Mona started her career as a soubrette in the Fol-de-Rols. They were celebrating (I think) a milestone anniversary and using the trip as a sort of working holiday, often staying in different hotels, and seldom mixing with the rest of the company.

This was the only one of my eight tours when the itinerary took us up to Katmandu in Nepal. We flew up there in a Fokker Friendship, a Dutch plane which has the wings above the fuselage and therefore excellent, unobstructed views from the windows. The Friendship was too small to fly over the mountains, so would fly up the valleys, curling round the peaks at the top - allowing wonderful views of the green paddy fields layered into the sides of the mountains. And then, as you rounded the final peak for the descent into Katmandu's valley, there was that thrill of the first, unmistakeable, sight of Everest in the distance.

Members of the company with time on their hands - and there were several - were given permission to spend days away when not required, so we were never quite sure who was in the hotel and who wasn't. Playing Bentley Summerhays in *Misalliance* was former child actor Andrew Ray, son of comedian Ted Ray and brother of television's musical personality Robin. Quite late on in the tour we discovered that he had been spending much of his free time smoking pot in ashrams in both Sri Lanka and India, with people such as Arthur C Clarke, the science fiction writer. He was so often away that no-one missed him on our final date of the tour when he was scheduled to appear in *Misalliance*: enquiries revealed that he had checked out of the hotel the previous evening and flown to Rhodesia in an attempt to patch things up with his estranged wife. I suppose in a way it justified Equity's insistence on understudies: one of them actually did perform on the last night of a very strange tour. Nothing stranger than being asked by the Bombay theatre people, who had forced the choice, why we had brought such a tedious play as *Misalliance*.

My first tour, with the Bristol Old Vic, ended in Sri Lanka - or Ceylon as it then was. I've been back many times since, and am still enthralled by the beauty of the country and the warmth of its people. Our 1963 performances were in a girl's school in Colombo; in a Jesuit College just outside Kandy, and in Jaffna Town Hall. The last was the most difficult for Liz and me as there was a hardboard ceiling covering the stage, with no way to hang our curtains and lights. We solved the problem by drilling dozens of small holes through the hardboard, passing our lines through the holes and hanging everything from the roof girders above.

What seemed to shock the locals more than our desecration of their Town Hall was the sight of an English memsahib (Liz) wearing jeans and clambering up and down ladders. We had considerable technical assistance from a Colombo theatre expert, Mahinda Dias. He had a small stock of equipment which he would pile into his old truck and, with half-a-dozen young technicians perched on top, drive all over the island doing fit-ups - both in halls and in the open air - for the Sri Lankan theatre groups. He loved helping the visiting groups, so it was a great pleasure to return his hospitality and to show him around some of the West End theatres when he came to London. One of his assistants, H D Saratchandra Perera, known to everyone as Sarat, worked with me on all of my tours and became a good friend. His eldest son, whom I first saw as a baby, was driving one of those noisy little three-wheel taxis in Colombo by the time of my last visit.

I have worked in forty-two countries - and visited many others - and am often asked which is my favourite. An impossible question to answer; each country has its attractions and its disadvantages, its good points and its bad points, but Sri Lanka would certainly rank very high on my list despite all the horrors of the civil war. Breathtaking scenery, warm friendly people (when they are not fighting each other) and an easy relaxed life-style: in fact I liked it so much that, when I became eligible for early retirement, I tried to buy a small hotel there.

Chapter Thirteen: Richelieu.

The Sri Lankan hotel didn't happen. I found a suitable property south of Colombo towards Mount Lavinia, and my budget would have covered purchase and renovation - but not the huge 'bond' which the government insisted that I, as a foreign national should deposit in a local bank. However, the hotel idea wouldn't go away. Back in Britain, someone suggested France: "It's in the EEC so no problems about nationality or work permits or transfer of money; you speak some French; why not a French hotel?" And that is why, during these early chapters I have been driving around western France looking at available or potential hotels. Not surprisingly, there were a great many: large and small; old and even older; in cities and villages, on main squares and in back streets. Some struggling to stay open and in desperate need of some tender loving care. Others long closed, often deservedly so. There were a few that justified a second look: the Mayor of Montignac's Donjon Hotel, for example; that certainly might have had some potential had his development of the racetrack and sports facilities been further advanced.

One day, venturing north towards the Loire Valley to inspect yet another hotel, I passed through an archway giving access to a walled village laid out in a symmetrical pattern around two main squares. The sun was shining: in the first of the squares a neoclassical church faced an attractive timbered market hall across a bustling market. I parked the car and introduced myself to the historic, picturesque village of Richelieu.

Cardinal Armand Jean Duplessis, Duke of Richelieu (1585-1642) had asked architect Jacques Lemercier to build a splendid Chateau on the site of his ancestral home, and used his great wealth to fill it with expensive art treasures: paintings by Titian, Rubens and van Dyck, and sculptures by Michelangelo.

The magnificent building was seized in 1792, and pulled down after the Revolution: you get a hint of the grandeur of the original scheme from the few remaining pavilions and the orangery nestling among the canals in parklands which now belong to the University of Paris. Sculptor Étienne-Jules Ramey's marble statue of Cardinal Richelieu graces the small square separating the Park from one of the three surviving town gates. This gate leads onto a *Grande Rue* lined with twenty-eight imposing '*hotels*', built as town houses for Richelieu's private court. Unfortunately the Cardinal died before construction was completed, so the courtiers never actually took up residence in what la Fontaine described as "this handsome but badly-sited village".

In 1607 Richelieu had been appointed Bishop of Lucon, an appointment which required the Pope's consent as Richelieu was underage at the time. His religious zeal in that post led, in 1615, to an appointment as Chaplain to the new Queen, Anne of Austria, and a year later an impressed King Louis XIII made him Secretary of War and Foreign Affairs. There were some tricky periods, including a spell in exile with the Queen Mother, Marie de Medicis, but he returned to the Court in triumph as Chief Minister to the King, then added the Cardinal's robes - and he ended his life acknowledged as one of the greatest politicians in European history. His founding of the strong 'nation-state' and his aggressive foreign policy during the period of the '30-year war' set the ground-rules for international politics for generations to come - although he made many enemies in the process.

Richelieu was a cultured man - he had a superb library (transferred to the Sorbonne in 1660) and was instrumental in the establishment of *L'Academie Francaise* - but also a sick man. A very sick man. He suffered from strangury and intestinal tuberculosis with fistula; his right arm suppurated with tubercular osteitis, and he coughed blood. Yet, somehow, in amongst all his handicaps and accomplishments and romantic liaisons he had found time to commission the village which would become my home for the next four years.

I suspect that every community has someone who knows his or her way around the system; who makes things happen; who gets things done. It didn't take long to discover Richelieu's 'Mr Fixit' since every *A Vendre* sign carried the same name, that of the local solicitor and estate agent Pierre Gravel. *Maître* Gravel's warm and friendly manner did not quite hide his clear determination to see me settled in a village property within a matter of hours rather than days. None of the three village hotels was officially 'on the market' but that wouldn't prevent Fixit Gravel showing me around the following morning so I checked into one of the three, but ate at a bar/restaurant on the *rue Henri Proust* which was where I first made the acquaintance of Daniel Dangeant, mine host of *l'Impérial* and quite possibly the most laid-back character that I've ever met. Outstandingly so, even in France which has more than its fair share of laid-back characters.
"What's on the menu tonight, Daniel?"
"*Surprise*".
"For me or for you?"
"*Pour tout le monde*", and he would then retreat to the kitchen and examine the contents of the fridge-freezer. Invariably one was offered *bif-steak*. Sometimes *bif-steak frites*, sometimes *bif-steak salade*. But in the right mood he was a capable chef and dinner was genuinely '*une surprise delicieuse*'.

His live-in lady friend was the charming, jolly Marie-Thérèse who worked as a relief Post Office manager by day and thus felt entitled to put her feet up in the evenings - the bar, after all, was Daniel's business. But she would occasionally put in an appearance, and even help out if the bar was particularly busy. Daniel's English was quite good and Richelieu's few expat residents were always made welcome. I remember once pulling into a Routier for a beer on the way south and being asked if I had driven down from Calais. "Yes" I said. "Then you'll know the way back" said the barman who had still not forgiven the British for deserting them at Dunkirk. Happily, Daniel's relaxed, if sometimes chaotic, management style defused any such antagonism.

The following morning *Maître* Gravel didn't waste much time on the hotel visits: the 3-star *Hotel Le Puits Doré* was clearly too big; the 3-bedroomed *Hotel LaPlâtre* clearly too small, and the huge, dusty, long-closed *Hotel Faisan* on the main square clearly a non-starter: like an old provincial railway hotel its creaky corridors and stairs occupied more floor space than the rooms. However, *Maître* Gravel knew his Napoleon: "the English are a nation of shop-keepers" and, without even checking my interest, had arranged for me to look at a corner shop just inside the gateway leading to Richelieu's statue and the Park, and close to the Market Square. Location, location, location. That box seemed to be ticked. A decent sized shop, with a good frontage and window. Another tick. Accommodation upstairs needed some attention, but less than any hotel I had looked at. The first question obviously had to be "Why is she selling?", but a quick look around her stock - postcards and gifts - made it obvious that she was totally dependent on visitors. As with any small seaside or tourist resort Richelieu had three months of trade and nine months of misery. I felt that expanded stock lines aimed at the residents rather than the visitors (and better displayed) could improve out-of-season turnover. Income from a shop would obviously be much less than from a hotel, but the overheads would be lower and staff requirements almost nil.

A few days later we had all shaken hands on the deal; *Maître* Fixit had arranged my residence permit - and submitted his invoice. I was in business, or would be as soon as I had a name for the shop. I wanted to call it The Corner

Shop, but there is no equivalent in French so we settled on *L'Encoignure*, the corner cupboard. I soon got to know the neighbours. From the shop opposite mine M. Lavigne sold cycles and mopeds and did welding on the side which was occasionally helpful. We always knew when one of the village lads (or, indeed, one of the lasses) had attained the age of fifteen as they would turn up at M Lavigne's shop with their fathers to select their very first moped. The youngest of the Lavigne's three children, Samuel, allowed me to 'help' him with his English homework - until the day he got poor marks for a translation (into English!) and decided to rely on his elder brother instead.

Richelieu

Next door (across a courtyard) was the home of Madame Colette Decock, who had been living near Bordeaux with her parents and two sisters when the Nazis invaded. Their men were all shipped away to the labour camps, leaving the women to run the farms on their own. They had a very hard time of it, and to this day Mme Decock finds it difficult to forgive the Germans. She's a tough lady. She moved to Richelieu when she married and, with her husband, ran the garage in the corner of the Market Square. Petrol, sales and repairs - seven days a week. And then, after just a few months, he was killed in a road accident: she was left to run the business and bring up her baby daughter, Janine, all on her own. By the time I took over the shop Janine was living in Orleans with two daughters, and no sign of a husband. The petrol pumps had disappeared, and the garage business was leased to a mechanic, but Madame Decock still lived in her splendid apartment above the garage. She was a regular visitor to my shop, but not as a customer.

"Monsieur Freeland, j'ai un petit problème", she would say, expecting me to close the shop immediately and sort out her little problem, whether it was simply to carry her gas bottle upstairs, or to re-plaster an entire bathroom wall. Demanding, but generous: she was an excellent cook and there was often a meal waiting when the chores were finished. Once she watched me very carefully while I was eating, and only at the end of the meal admitted that she had fed me horsemeat, unsure how *l'anglais* would react. I had actually guessed: it is grainier and tougher than beef, but perfectly acceptable.

Her two sisters would often visit: one from their family home down south and the other from her married home in the capital: they were known to us both as *Madame de Bordeaux* and *Madame de Paris*. I still get Christmas cards from them, and an 'annual report' on the current state of play in Richelieu scribbled in Madame Decock's increasingly spidery handwriting. A good Catholic lady who only permitted *deux bisous* (two kisses) from her single neighbour, rather than the usual three. Even after four years I was not allowed to use the diminutive *tu*, but always *vous*."*Tu* is for family, and people you've slept with" she explained.

It was through Madame Decock that I came to know the other Sisters, the nuns from the neoclassical church on the west side of the Square. Their 'convent' was a nice little house behind the Market Hall, and I was often bidden to dine with them. No problems with *bisous* there, and the proffered bottles of wine were enjoyed without any sign of guilt - but I never risked a "*tu*". Their priest also enjoyed a drink or three at the *Bar l'Impérial*. He, I suspect, had also suffered at the hands of the Nazis, and his favourite story involved the Nazi Commander waiting to invade England. Not having any ships, he lines his soldiers up along the beach and orders "Trinken; trinken". Across the Channel the English commander sees the water level dropping, lines his men up on the beach and orders "Pissen; pissen".

I was invited to join the village *Chambre de Commerce* just around the time they decided to start a *Foire aux Vins*, a wine fair in and around the Cardinal's old Orangery, one of the few remaining buildings in his Park. Chinon is just a few miles north of Richelieu, and the Chinon red wine was then our everyday choice, but generally speaking the local wines were not great: you had to go further north to the Loire valley for a half-decent red (St Nicolas de Bourgueil) or an extremely decent white Vouvray. Present day 'experts' (ie: most of the French and all of the English) agree that the Chinon red has improved, and is now possibly better than the Bourgueil. Whichever, dealers from as far away as Anjou and Saumur were happy to rent trade spaces in the park and our *Foire aux Vins* proved to be the first of many.

Incidentally, the town of Chinon is built around the Chateau in which Peter O'Toole and Katharine Hepburn battled it out as Henry II and Eleanor of Aquitaine in the 1968 film *The Lion In Winter*. When that film first opened in England they arranged a special midnight screening for casts and staff of the West End theatres. The place was packed. At the end of their great argument, when Miss Hepburn drags herself up the doorpost and, in that husky voice, drawled "I guess every family has it's little ups and downs" the cinema erupted: the cheering and applause totally drowned out the next few minutes of dialogue.

The *Foire aux Vins* certainly boosted trade in my shop over that busy weekend. To the tourist tat and postcards I had added birthday and Christmas cards, a wide range of British foodstuffs (including a large selection of Cottage Delight) and Scottish soaps and handicrafts in my efforts to develop out-of-season trade: I even arranged mail order kilts and tartan culottes. As long as the exchange rate held, the shop was covering costs. I was accepted within the village. I learnt the French names for everything on the shelves. I also learned to recognise the dodgy commercial travellers, the thieves and the chancers: once when I was busy and the shop was full I thought I saw a lady pick something up from a shelf but not replace it. When she didn't show it at the till I challenged her - nervously, because I knew that everyone was watching and listening. I had no proof, just a sixth sense. She denied it. I insisted - and she then suddenly 'remembered'; took it out of her pocket and paid for it. Phew!

Its history meant that this handsome but badly-sited village was regularly included in the holiday guides. The Daily Telegraph's Travel Writer wrote in one of his French features that "Richelieu has its own little Marks and Spencer, presided over by a friendly Englishman" and, generally speaking, I had a good relationship with the villagers. Certainly Richelieu must have had a higher proportion of tartan kilts and culottes per head of population than any other village in France. I got involved in village events, and personally organised an annual Collector's Market in the *Salle des Fétes*. I was delighted that so many of the villagers remembered me on this return visit - and that Madame Decock had lunch waiting for me when I arrived.

Madame Decock's annually-scrawled epistles had prepared me for some of the changes in Richelieu during my long absence, but there was one major surprise. My little Corner Cupboard had completely disappeared to be subsumed into the redeveloped *Hotel Le Puits Doré*; a magnificent reconstruction which has really smartened up that particular corner of the village. Olivier Blanc, the present owner, gave me a guided tour. What used to be my home, storeroom and attic are now luxury hotel bedrooms - in fact, I spent that night in a most comfortable bed in what had once been my attic. Entire staircases have been removed; floors have been raised or lowered to improve access through to the original hotel, and a lift has been installed with its ground floor access in a corner of my former shop.

In a village where other small businesses are clearly struggling, the *Hotel Le Puits Doré* and its restaurant are well on the way to recovering the one million euros investment, in large part due to the charm, talents and efficiency of its *patron*. In other parts of the village the *Hotel LaPlâtre* is a private house; the *Faisan Hotel* remains forlornly empty, and the *Bar l'Impérial* is no more. I had the honour of being best man at the 1996 wedding of Marie-Thérèse to Daniel, mine host at *l'Impérial*, and had hoped to spend some time with them in their married home at Mignac but, sadly, they have just separated after twenty-nine years together. I had lunch with a disconsolate Marie-Thérèse in Chatellerault.

One event which has started since my departure, and become a successful annual attraction is an Antiques Fair, held in the old timbered Market Hall which is enclosed with colourful draperies and wonderfully illuminated for the occasion. (see photo on page 96). For the rest of the year the Market Hall houses the food stalls at the weekly *Marché*, and in my time was often used as a skateboard park by the village youngsters.

The preserved steam railway which, in happier days, operated a line from Richelieu through to Chinon is long closed. The trains have moved on: those tracks which have not been removed or filled in are rusting and overgrown with weeds. One hopes that the old station site, just a few minute's walk from the main square, will be opened up for commercial development. On a happier note, the *Foire aux Vins* - started during my time in the village - continues to attract big crowds every autumn.

Chapter Fourteen: From Saint-Simon to Sardinia.

Richelieu called itself *La Cité du Cardinal.* Saint-Simon, a little village on the north bank of the Charente between Angoulême and Jarnac, is famous as the *Village des Gabarriers'.* Saint-Simon is said to be named after Saint Sigismund, the King of Burgundy who was assassinated in 524AD and later canonised - with his remains transferred to Prague where he is Patron Saint.

The Vikings invaded the region by dragging their flat-bottomed boats up the river - possibly as far as Civray. In the 11th century salt was being traded through Cognac on flat-bottomed, single-masted boats known as *gabarres* whose designs may well be based on their Viking predecessors. During the 16th and 17th centuries the village carpenters of

Saint-Simon specialised in the building and repair of these *gabarres*, and by the 19th century the village was accepted as the most important shipyard on a river which was the region's principal route for bulk transportation. Around 25% of all the boats operating on the Charente were based in Saint-Simon. *Gabarres* were used to move *eau-de-vie* from Jarnac and Cognac down to the port of Rochefort, and in 1666, when Colbert convinced King Louis XIV to develop a Rochefort base for his new French Navy, the stone and much of the armoury - including the 800 cannon from Ruelle - travelled there on board the *gabarres*. In the peak year, 1892, the total registered cargo carried on these boats was 7.6 million tons - although the trade started to decline with the development of steam engines and the railways. The last *gabarre* sailed out of Jarnac in 1930. In 1800 the population of Saint-Simon was around 700: today it is little more than 250, but it remains 'the village of the *gabarriers*'. The shipyard is again operational: they have built a facsimile *gabarre* which cruises daily on the Charente during the summer months. A similar boat operates daily from the quay at Cognac, and you can cruise on more modern boats from Angouléme's Port de l'Houmeau or hire holiday cruisers from Le Boat in Jarnac.

Apart from a couple of holidays on the Norfolk Broads and numerous ferry crossings of the Channel, my only sea-going experience was a curious summer cruising the Mediterranean as Entertainments Manager for Clarkson's Holidays. They had leased a Greek cruise liner for the summer, the MV Delphi. We picked up our holidaymakers each Friday at Naples, and took them on a round trip to Sicily, Malta, Tunis, Sardinia, Civitavecchia (for Rome) and then back to Naples where the coaches returned them to the airport and replaced them with the following week's boat-load of pale British sun-seekers. So what was 'curious' about that, I hear you asking? There were several holiday firms offering similar packages. Yes, there were, but the two at the lower end of the market, Clarkson's and Thomson's, were in serious competition.

Thomson's had bought other rival companies - Skytours, Riviera, Luxitours and Britannia Airways - but continued to run them as independent units and their internal rivalry allowed Clarkson's to become the lead player. In 1971 Thomson's formed a new Board, appointed a new Chairman and Chief Executive and re-launched all these units as a single company known as Thomson Holidays. Television advertising and drastic price cutting (4 nights in Majorca for £19) grabbed the public's imagination, and the increased business was threatening rival firms Clarkson's and Horizon.

This, then, was the situation when I joined MV Delphi in the spring of 1974. We collected the ship from Efthimiasis Lines in Piraeus and sailed via the Corinth Canal to Naples where we picked up our first passengers all eager for a week of sunshine and bingo and baked alaska pudding. The Delphi sailed overnight, docked early morning, and soon after breakfast the passengers would be despatched on coaches to savour the delights of, in turn, Catania, Valetta, Tunis, Cagliari, Rome and Naples. Practically forced onto the coaches, because it soon became known that the competition from Thomson's along with high inflation, the sinking pound and rising fuel costs was forcing our Company to sell holidays at £1 less than cost. The profit from the coach tours was the only thing keeping Clarkson's 'afloat'.

While our passengers were being guided around Sicily's port city of Catania and admiring the view of Mount Etna in the distance, I dashed up the coast to revisit Taormina, a stunningly beautiful little town with the ruins of a Roman amphitheatre, and pleasant open air cafes fitted into narrow terraces overlooking the blue waters. My main memory of our next stop, Valetta, is also theatrical; the chance to visit the jewel that is the Manoel Theatre, a miniature Italianate-style opera house, although the busy harbour and the city's many other attractions made one want to spend more time on that charming, friendly island.

I could happily have spent a whole week in Tunis with its attractive blue-washed buildings, and sun-drenched history, but Tunis also had a more modern tourist attraction - the sets built for Franco Zeffirelli's film, Jesus of Nazareth which, in 1974, was proving a rival attraction to the city's mosques and souks.

I didn't see as much of Sardinia as I should have done. On a compact vessel such as the Calypso you are with the passengers pretty much all of the time. You eat with them in the dining room; drink with them in the bars and ballroom, and meet them on the decks or in the public areas. They always have something to say, usually complimentary but not always, so sometimes it is relief when they disappear on the coach tours and you can relax for a while. On one of our days in Sardinia the relaxation was ended by a panic phone call: the guide on one of the coaches couldn't speak English and the passengers were "not happy". I was despatched in a taxi to sort things out, although since I didn't understand Italian and she didn't speak English I wasn't too sure what I could do to help. When I got there "not happy" proved a bit of an understatement: the smell of revolution filled the bus. Fortunately both the guide and I had a bit of French, so she fed me the information in broken French and I translated it into what I hoped was a running commentary on our tour around Cagliari. On our way to our final attraction, a vineyard where there would be tastings of some of Sardinia's modestly-pleasant wines, we passed the Delphi in the harbour. I worked into the commentary that "on your right you can see the best cruise ship in the Mediterranean" and got a big cheer, so the worst seemed to be over. The smiles and the clinking of bottles when they eventually returned to the ship suggested that the rescue operation had been successful.

I suppose that the long coach drive from Civitavecchia to Rome is worth it if that is your first, or your one and only, visit to that great city, but for me Rome deserves more than three or four pinched hours. You really need to 'absorb' Rome. Happily I had been there before so I only did that coach trip once, just for the experience. The final leg of the cruise took the Delphi back to Naples where it seemed to be overcast and wet almost every Friday, making the lines of laundry slung between the buildings across every side street look depressingly grey. No sign of depression on the Delphi, however. Off went the lights, and the passengers celebrated the last night of their Mediterranean cruise, cheering the waiters as they paraded around the dining room holding up their flaming baked alaskas.

We did several weeks aboard this 'Butlins on Sea' before the Delphi went off on charter for the high season. We were contracted to return for more circular cruises in the late summer/autumn, but that never happened. Court Line, the air travel operators who had taken over Clarkson's, collapsed with debts of over £7million in what Flight International described as "the most spectacular failure in package holiday history". They estimated that in the five years previous to the collapse, eight million holidays had been sold at an average £1 below cost with the obvious and inevitable result. We were invited to lodge a claim for loss of earnings but what was the point? There wasn't any money. So - another theatre tour, perhaps? Time to head back to London Town.

Chapter Fifteen: From Jarnac to Juhu.

Next town on the Charente is Jarnac, home of the Courvoisier wine and spirit warehouse (*chai*) with its foyer exhibition containing some of Napoleon's coats and hats. The Emperor had so enjoyed their cognac brandy that he appointed Courvoisier his sole supplier but, dominant though it is, Courvoisier is not the only distiller in Jarnac. You can find Thomas Hine there, as well as Louis Royer and others. The former President, Francois Mitterand, was born in Jarnac, and the town has two adjoining Museums dedicated to him. The *Donation Francois Mitterand* contains all the gifts presented to him by other Heads of State. There are many superb paintings and engravings (including a Piranesi) on the walls surrounding a bizarre and varied collection of objects, notably two magnificent dragons from the King of Nepal and (my favourites) two splendid jewelled sabres. The *Musée des Maquettes* has models and photographs of major architectural projects undertaken in Paris during his two periods in office. As a theatre man I was particularly fascinated by the model and plans of the Bastille Opera House.

The region also produces *Pineau des Charentes*, a liqueur wine made from three parts grape juice to one part cognac. Drunk chilled as an aperitif or dessert wine, *pineau* comes in two varieties - dry white and a fruitier rose. According to the legend, a winemaker accidentally decanted grape juice into a barrel containing *eau-de-vie*. Later, after the mixture had fermented, the end product was found to be so pleasant that the result was developed into *pineau* as we know it today. My lunch at the *Marmite* in Mansle had offered as a starter half a Charentais melon filled with *pineau*: highly recommended.

Three strange facts.....
1. Only 3% of all cognac produced is actually drunk in France: the rest is exported.
2. The early consumers and, indeed, the early producers, were not French but British and Irish, which is why the grades are in English for example: VSOP- Very Superior Old Pale).
3. The equivalent of 20 million bottles of cognac are lost every year due to evaporation from the oak casks. This loss is known as 'The Angel's Share'.

All this talk of alcohol reminds me of one of my more difficult Indian tours, my first as company and tour manager. The show was a little two-hander called *Dear Liar* developed from the correspondence between George Bernard Shaw and Mrs Patrick Campbell. Their contracted tour manager had pulled out three days before departure and I was quickly drafted in - meeting the two performers for the first time at Heathrow Airport check-in. Before we had even passed through customs she had whispered to me "You'd better watch David: he drinks". In the departure lounge he sidled up and hissed "You'll need to keep an eye on Eithne: she carries a bottle of gin in her handbag". Ah well, at least that solved the question "Why had the previous manager given up a golden opportunity to tour India?" They were professional enough not to over-indulge before a performance, but the after-show receptions were a nightmare.

Word gets around, and actors who drink find it increasingly difficult to find work: they become unreliable, and the drink interferes with their ability to learn and remember lines. Despite a wonderfully deep voice and an imposing stage presence, David ended up in a care home. Eithne, after a long period of 'resting', announced her retirement and moved back to Ireland. At her farewell party she told us all "there's nothing left for me here. It's all over; you won't see me in London again". "And if any enquiries should come in?" asked her agent. "I'll be on the next plane back".

That *Dear Liar* tour is packed with memories: because of the circumstances, I had never seen their show. Not even a rehearsal. And their first performance was on a stage so tiny that the stage manager operated from behind the back curtain rather than in the wings, so I never actually saw the show I was stage managing until the second venue. In Pakistan we lunched with the British High Commissioner: arriving a few minutes early we were ushered into his office where the works of art covering his walls included what appeared to be a small signed Picasso. Over lunch I asked him if it was genuine. "Oh, do we have a Picasso?" he asked. "I hadn't noticed". We also lunched with the High Commissioner in India, Sir John Freeman, the former television presenter (*Face To Face*). He sent his car to collect us from the hotel - the longest car I have ever been in. There was only one other guest at the lunch - the News Chronicle reporter James Cameron - and we sensibly sat and listened while these two great journalists discussed the current Indian situation (this was less than twenty years after Independence). They knew so much, had seen so much, and understood so much. I bet either would have noticed if he had a Picasso hanging above the office fireplace. In that same room on a later tour I met another of the world's great journalists, Sir Mark Tully, the BBC's Indian correspondent.

All three were reporters of the Indian scene, but on my last trip to India I was a guest of one of the participants involved in the negotiations leading up to Independence, Badr-ud-Din Tyabji, a Bombay-born Muslim.

"The advice given me by a senior colleague in my early days had sunk deep into my consciousness" he wrote. *"Never refuse a post"*. He moved to Delhi as Deputy Secretary in the new Planning and Development Department set up by Lord Wavell, the then Viceroy, to plan and carry out schemes for relief and reconstruction after the war, and prepare for post-war development".

That Department was wound up in 1946, and Mr Tyabji was appointed Deputy Secretary of the new Constituent Assembly. *"An administrative role, hence onerous and exacting"*. One of his responsibilities would be the conversion of the old Central Library Hall into a 600-seat Chamber for the new Assembly. *"This post gave me an excellent opportunity to follow the momentous, almost hectic, negotiations that were going on about the future of India. I renewed my acquaintance with Pandit Nehru, Mr Jinnah and Mahatma Ghandi: I had known them all for years, although I had no kind of personal rapport with Mr Jinnah who had been at the Inns of Court in London with my father. As a law student I had liked and admired Mr Jinnah, but now - although courteous - he always brushed aside my questions on how the creation of Pakistan would solve the minorities problem of the sub-continent"*.

Clement Atlee's success in the 1945 elections led to the appointment of Lord Mountbatten as Viceroy, sent out to India with only one charge - to deliver Independence. But what kind of settlement would there be, could there be, between the Indian National Congress and the Muslim League? As Secretary of the Minorities Committee, Badr-ud-Din Tyabji worked in close rapport with Sir Benegal Narsing Rau, the Constitutional Advisor:
"I conceived the highest admiration of his ability, integrity and gentlemanliness. Through this rather special equation I got to know - and in some degree to influence - a far wider field of the issues involved in Constitution-making than were

strictly covered by the definition of my duties. Sir B N Rau's views were much more in harmony with those of Pandit Nehru than those of Sardar Patel; the dichotomy in the approaches of the two most powerful leaders of the Congress party was patently weakening the government and the administration, and dividing the Civil Service".

Lord Mountbatten's special Advisor was V P Menon who had risen through the ranks without a cosmopolitan education or experience in the Civil Service or High Court, and who *"was now in the highest counsels of the government where independent judgement based on principles unconnected with personal advance was required. The advice that he gave, and the proposals that he made to Lord Mountbatten regarding the Partition seemed to me to have been misconceived.*

It was not for me to argue for or against the procedure followed for British withdrawal from India, and the partitioning of Bengal and the Punjab. However, I do wish to record the dismay, disillusionment and anxiety I felt as old friendships disintegrated in the face of personal ambitions, affecting the destiny of millions for generations to come. The split between Sardar Patel's strong-arm tactics, and the believers in the more flexible, accommodating and liberal outlook of Pandit Nehru, was complete. One was in favour of a clean break with Pakistan; the other sought to keep the options open so that time, experience, geography and language might bring them closer together at some later date.

Nehru and Ghandi seemed to me the only two leaders in whom an Indian Muslim could, unreservedly, place his faith. They went about the country rallying the broken-down feeling of the left-over minorities, risking their lives to inspire faith in the new India that would come into being, whatever happened across the border. And as the day of freedom from British rule drew nearer, physical violence of the most brutal kind between the two sides became the order of the day.

I had to get my guns out for protection against the mobs of gangsters who were breaking into every unguarded Muslim home, looting it, and often killing the inhabitants. We soon decided that my wife and children should go to Hyderabad to stay with my wife's parents. The drive to the airport in a military jeep was an experience in itself: one was constantly hearing of Muslim families being killed while making that same journey. The Delhi police force had virtually disintegrated: most of its Muslim officers had left, or opted for Pakistan; Muslims in other ranks feared for their lives".

Tyabji accepted an offer of accommodation with a Punjabi friend Chaman Lall, and two days later his own house was broken into and looted, one of the looters being an armed Sikh soldier who claimed to be guarding the house. Nehru heard of the break-in, visited the house, and chalked his initials on the remaining boxes - instructing the police officers to take good care of them, and Tyabji " *felt again that I was an accepted member of the Indian family*".

The Indian Assembly met at midnight on 14/15 August 1947 when Lord Mountbatten's announcement of India's Independence, Nehru's Tryst with Destiny oration, and the unfurling of the new national flag, ended Mr Tyabji's considerable involvement with the Constituent Assembly. Lady Mountbatten herself described the unfurling: *"The ceremony was typically Indian. The most intricate details had been checked by Louis himself, but when we arrived there were huge crowds, well over half-a-million, with the places where we were supposed to sit occupied by villagers. The carriage could not get near the flagpole".*

And Lord Mountbatten:

"The crush was terrible. At one moment a mother standing near to us could find no safe place for her baby and passed it up into the carriage. Edwina smiled, and held it tight. Eventually we had to hoist the flag from a large distance using tied string".

Badr-ud-din Tyabji moved on to the Foreign Service - as India's representative in Belgium. This was the first time that his wife Surayya had been out of India but she quickly learned both conversational French, and the intricacies of ordering and serving alcoholic drinks at receptions and dinners (prohibition was still in force in India and, officially, at least, in the overseas Embassies).

Father, on his wedding day.

Son, in his one-man-show

Surayya had sadly died shortly before my 1990 visit to the Tyabji household in New Delhi where Badr-ud-Din lived with his daughter Laila and his youngest son Khalid, who had engineered the invitation. Khalid had been a student at the National Academy of Drama, an actor, a budding director and writer, and in 1970 he had been engaged by the British Council to keep an eye on one of our drama tours while we were in the capital. One afternoon he turned up with complimentary tickets for a gallery opening, and invited me to join him. I don't remember any of the pictures (perhaps there were some of Surayya's, she was an accomplished artist) but I do remember the non-stop conversation as we strolled around the gallery and Khalid spoke to me about the death of his mother - something which, I believe, he had not previously discussed with anyone.

We kept in touch (he was at that time planning a research trip to Bihar) and met up again on my next drama tour to the sub-continent. By 1990 I had finished touring, and was making what was probably my last trip to the sub-continent. I had failed with negotiations to take over the little hotel in Sri Lanka and was invited to stay with the Tyabji's in Delhi on my way home. The third Test Match between England and India was being played at the Oval and, in a break with usual family rules, the radio was left on during meals. On the last day of my visit David Gower was scoring well in the second innings: An overnight flight; underground train and bus to the Oval in time to see not just Gower's century, but a wonderful flowing innings of 157 not out as England held on for a draw. (India had scored 606 in the first innings).

Khalid was always more interested in contemporary drama. He came to London with a one-man-show quite unlike anything I've ever attempted, and went off to work in Poland where he met Jola, an actress married to Zbigniew Cynkutis, a principal actor with Grotowski at the Laboratorium. Cynkutis died in a plane crash in 1987 leaving a trunk-full of notes which Khalid and Jola turned into a book *Acting with Grotowski*. Khalid and Jola married and enjoyed 16 years of joint performances before she died of advanced cancer. Khalid has since translated that book; his English version was published by Routledge in 2015 with the sub-title *Theatre as a Field for Experiencing Life*. Khalid remains busy, teaching at the National Academy of Drama and planning yet another one-man-show. Correspondence is sporadic, but always enlivening.

One final memory of that *Dear Liar* tour is an unforgettable chance meeting with the most incredible couple; Geoffrey Kendal and his wife Laura Liddell. A reminder for anyone who doesn't immediately recognise their names: they were the stars of a Merchant-Ivory film *Shakespeare Wallah*, based loosely on their real-life experiences touring Indian schools and villages with their own Anglo-Indian company *Shakespeareana* presenting cut-down productions of classic British dramas, but you may know them better as the parents of that lovely actress Felicity Kendal.

I had met up with Geoffrey and Laura, quite by chance, at the Breach Candy open air swimming pool in Bombay (now Mumbai), and had such a fascinating chat that we almost forgot to swim. Both of them were born in the Lake District: Geoffrey (Bragg) went to school in Kendal (adopted as his stage name) and they met while touring with the Edward Dunstan Company. "Dunstan was the best actor I have ever seen anywhere" Geoffrey wrote in his very readable biography *Shakespeare Wallah*, "but his company had money problems and folded in 1933". The young lovers went off to Gretna Green and got married.

Managements were reluctant to employ 'couples', so they borrowed £200 from their respective parents and set up the Bragg-Liddell Company which toured England and Scotland with Laura playing leading roles until a few weeks prior to the arrival of Jennifer in February 1934. Jennifer later recalled *"I was raised among so many period costumes and make-ups, but I remember only a total feeling of security as long as there lurked the smells of theatre, grease-paint, dust and the perspiration of terrified actors"*.

There were unhappy tours with H V Nielson; happy tours with Ben Greet, and repertory work at Bedford in 1939 until the declaration of war closed all the theatres. Geoffrey volunteered in the Merchant Navy, but was soon transferred to ENSA and acted with Laura in a tour of *Gaslight* - first in Britain, and then in India where the Bombay officer in charge of ENSA was Colonel Jack Hawkins, the future film star. According to Geoffrey "A better man for the job could not have been found anywhere". They toured widely, travelling in a private railway coach as far as Darjeeling in the north east, and the tribal territories of the north west frontier. Eventually Laura's second pregnancy forced them to return home, and Felicity arrived in September 1946. With the war over, an ex-ENSA colleague Peter Meriton suggested that they form a repertory company to tour in India which, with the encouragement and help of a Nawab of Hyderabad, they did, travelling out on the liner Strathmore in the winter of 1946/47.

"The news that an English company was coming to Trivandrum to stage some of the plays of Shakespeare was like dropping manna in the way of starved people. We attended the theatre every day, and found in such profusion answers to the questions which confronted us when trying to visualise an action when reading a play. We thank you for having given us so much knowledge about Shakespeare and his plays".

They were still touring in India at the time of Independence (15 August 1947) and the assassination of Gandhi (2 February 1948). Watching his ashes carried out to sea, they decided it was time to return to Britain.

They toured Ireland for a year, did Rep in Redditch (Felicity had her first walk-on part as a fairy), more rep in 1951/52 (with Jennifer playing the cockney girl in *The Corn is Green*), and then, during a frantic three-week season of repertory in Malta, their shows were seen by the Earl and Countess Mountbatten. At Edwina Mountbatten's suggestion, Nehru invited the Company to return to India. They arrived in Bombay in June 1953, did several performances in schools and military barracks, and were invited to a performance of *Deewar* (Wall) starring the classical Indian actor Prithviraj Kapoor - an evening which proved to be the beginning of a long relationship between their two families. Prithvi's son, Shashi, soon joined the Kendal's *Shakespeareana* company. For the first time, the Kendal's two daughters were touring with them. Felicity started her career as a young ASM alongside her elder sister, Jennifer, by now an established actress. Jennifer fell in love and married Shashi, who became a major film star, but never lost his love of the theatre.

Shashi and Jennifer Kapoor with family

Shakespeareana continued to tour until 1962. *Shakespeare Wallah* was filmed in 1963; Merchant and Ivory encouraged Felicity to try her luck in London. Jennifer was raising children and performing with the Prithvi Theatre Group in Juhu, so Geoffrey and Laura settled in Goa (not too far from the grandchildren). I saw one of their little 'recital tours', and thought that Laura spoke verse as beautifully as any English actress. The two of them had spent a huge part of their lives doing exactly what I was then doing for just ten or twelve weeks at a time, and we were even able to compare notes on some of the venues. Moreover they had done it largely at their own expense, whereas I was getting a salary from the British Council. I learned so much from them, and have never forgotten that meeting. Geoffrey and Laura came to see our production of *Dear Liar* that evening and, within a few weeks of our departure, they were on stage as Bernard Shaw and Mrs Patrick Campbell in their own version of this same play.

"Shashi is mad" Jennifer wrote to Felicity, by then (1974) settled in London; "he wants to build a theatre". In fact it was Jennifer who worked alongside architect Ved Segan designing an experimental 200-seat theatre which had the audience seated on three sides of an octagonal thrust stage. The Prithvi Theatre, named in honour of Shashi's father, opened 5th November 1978 in Juhu, just to the north of Mumbai.

On yet another Indian tour - as stage manager with *Kemp's Jig*, the one-man-show featuring that talented actor, writer and pantomime dame the late Chris Harris, we had a chance to work in this charming, intimate venue, with its superb acoustics. We also enjoyed afternoon tea with Jennifer and her children in their lovely Juhu home.

The photo shows Geoffrey and Laura performing *Dear Liar* in their daughter's Theatre in 1984, the same year that Jennifer sadly died of cancer. Since then management of the Prithvi Theatre has been taken over by the Kendal's grand-children, Jennifer's children, Sanjna and Kunal Kapoor.

Chapter Sixteen: With Max Adrian to Mildura

Bernard Shaw, through that production of his play *Man and Superman* at Bristol in 1957, had been indirectly responsible for my own start in theatre management. Over the next fifty-odd years, working on plays by and about him, working with people who knew him, and in two cases working with actors who had been directed by him, I developed an intense interest in Shaw the man which eventually led to my own solo performance *George Bernard Shaw: Playing The Clown* which has so occupied my recent years.

I must credit an actor, the talented, if somewhat unpredictable Max Adrian (one of his reviews even called him eccentric) for leading me towards *Playing The Clown*.

Max (family name: Bors) was born in Enniskillen in Northern Ireland and, aged 25, made his stage debut as a chorus dancer. He was in Tod Slaughter's Company, spent a year with Northampton Repertory Company, and was then cast in a production of Terence Rattigan's play *First Episode* which took him to London and Broadway. He returned to London to play The Dauphin in Shaw's *St Joan* (Old Vic 1939), and two roles with John Gielgud's Haymarket Company: Pandarus in *Troilus & Cressida*, and Sir Ralph Bonnington in *Doctor's Dilemma* (Shaw again).

After the war he switched from the classics to intimate revue - *Tuppence Coloured; Oranges & Lemons; Penny Plain; Airs on a Shoestring; From Here to There* and *Fresh Airs* - giving over 2000 performances, before playing Dr Pangloss on Broadway in Bernstein's *Candide* (short run, but the original cast recording was (still is) a best seller. Back to London (and Broadway) for Noel Coward's *Look After Lulu*, and then came a remarkable series of films for Ken Russell: *Song of Summer; The Music Lovers; The Boy Friend* and *The Devils*.

I had worked with Max at both the Royal Shakespeare Company and the National Theatre (he was a founder member of both) and I was asked by Martin Tickner if I would stage manage and light Max's touring one-man-show *An Evening with George Bernard Shaw*. There were some one-nighters in the north-east (oh, no) and - after a couple of week's filming with Ken Russell - a world tour opening in New Zealand (ah, yes, that's more like it). Martin was managing the British leg of the tour: the British Council, Australia Council and an Australian manager Cliff Hocking would be looking after the foreign dates.

Naturally, I said 'yes'. The British dates included a delightful sold out evening at the Aldburgh Festival for Ruth, Lady Fermoy, the Queen Mother's Lady-in-Waiting, and a near-empty, damp Sunday evening in the 2000-seat Sunderland Empire. That's show business.

Martin Tickner had rented a car for us and, after the final tour date, I had to take Max over to the Lake District for his location work on Ken Russell's TV film *Song of Summer* in which Max was playing the composer Delius. It had been arranged that I would stay the night there before taking the car back to London, and I was invited to join the cast and crew for dinner. Three weeks later Max and I were flying out to New Zealand, via Los Angeles and an overnight stop in Fiji. Our Auckland performances were part of the 1968 opening season of a new repertory company in a converted cinema, renamed The Mercury after Orson Welles' famous 1937 Theatre Group. We also did an enjoyable Q&A session with the local drama students before flying on to Australia. On arrival in Sydney we were met at the airport by the Australia Council representatives who drove us into the city, highlighting the places of interest along the route. Nearing the harbour they pointed out the Quantas Hotel "where the big stars stay when they are in Sydney", and I felt the temperature cooling in the car as we continued to drive over the famous bridge, and up into North Sydney where we pulled into a pleasant little Motel. A Motel deliberately chosen for our convenience as it was just around the corner from our venue, the Independent Theatre, but I sensed that Mr Max Adrian, founder member of the Royal Shakespeare Company and the National Theatre, with his name in lights on Broadway for *Candide* and *Look After Lulu* was not a happy bunny. It was a quiet dinner that evening, and when I went down for breakfast the next morning I discovered Max sitting in the lobby, bags packed, waiting for the taxi which would take him to the Quantas Hotel "where the big stars stay when they are in Sydney".

The Independent Theatre, formerly The Criterion and before that a winding station, had been run since 1930 by a formidable lady named Doris Fitton who managed and directed and acted and probably stuck up the posters and sold the tickets. She kept the organisation going until 1977 when her age and ill health, and the theatre's deteriorating finances, forced its closure. Max always referred to her as 'Old Doll Fitton'. There was certainly a touch of the Lillian Bayliss about her, but we were well looked after, and business was good. I enjoyed Sydney: it could have been a busy time for me as altered schedules meant some re-arrangements to our internal flights, but the efficient Paul Jellard at BOAC's Sydney office sorted things out so quickly that I made it to a matinee of the musical *Man of la Mancha* at Her Majesty's Theatre. I was overwhelmed by the show and by the production and have wanted to direct it ever since.

Starring in an Australian Broadcasting Company TV series at that time was the actor-singer Denis Quilley. I had seen him, of course, in the title role of *Candide* in my first experience of West End musicals, but Max had worked with him in *Airs on a Shoestring* at the Royal Court and arranged for the three of us to lunch at 'the hotel where the big stars stay when they are in Sydney'. Denis had gone out to Australia for a tour of *Robert and Elizabeth* with June Bronhill, and had then been cast as Inspector Hallam in what proved to be a successful, long-running series, *Contrabandits*, which he described as "Z-Cars by Sydney Bridge". With the series drawing to a close, he was planning to return to the UK but to what? He was rather concerned that his style of musicals had gone out of fashion.

Denis Quilley

Googie Withers

I was also invited to join Max for afternoon tea with actress Googie Withers in her charming harbour-side home with views across to the nearly-finished Opera House. Googie's husband, John McCallum, formerly a successful stage, TV and film actor in both Britain and Australia, was running the JC Williamson Theatre Company, universally known in show business as 'The Firm'. James Cassius Williamson, an American, first arrived in Australia as leading actor in a play scheduled for a 12-week tour, extended to fifteen months. He leased the Theatre Royal in Sydney, then made his fortune by buying the Australian rights to the Gilbert & Sullivan operas. 'The Firm' owned theatres, and world rights to many productions and films: John McCallum was their current Joint Managing Director. I should have loved to discuss theatre management with him, but at that time John was busy working on the second series of *Skippy the Bush Kangaroo*. Instead I tucked into the tea and cakes and sat enthralled as two 'old pros', Googie and Max, gossiped the afternoon away.

John and Googie often returned to the UK: Googie for the TV series *Within These Walls*, when she played the prison governor Faye Boswell, and together they appeared in several plays, notably Somerset Maugham's *The Circle* at Chichester, on tour and on Broadway. Both John and Googie were awarded CBEs in the UK and became Officers of the Order of Australia, Googie being the first non-Australian to be so honoured. Her last film was the 1996 award-winning *Shine* but she was back in the news in 2004 when Norris Cole, a character in the TV series *Coronation Street* said "Googie Withers would turn in her grave". In fact, she was still very much alive, and Granada Television was forced to offer an apology. She died in 2011, a year after John.

At my request our tour schedule included a brief visit to Hobart, Tasmania. Many years previously my cousin Cynthia and her ex-policeman husband Wilfred had emigrated from south London to Hobart, and the visit gave me a chance to meet up with them again. We were performing in the Theatre Royal, opened in 1836 and built, in part, with convict labour - it remains the oldest working theatre in Australia. Noel Coward called it "a dream of a theatre" but it was in a poor state in the 1940s. Demolition seemed likely until the recently-knighted Sir Laurence Olivier, on tour with an Old Vic Company, made an impassioned speech from the stage which encouraged the State Government to buy the building for £12,000, and to renovate it. There was a later $1 million renovation following a fire in 1984.

I fell in love with the theatre, and felt comfortable in the city: when the post of Theatre Manager was advertised some months later I put in an application and was interviewed at Australia House in London, but sadly didn't get the job. I've been turned down for plenty of jobs, but losing out on that one really was a major disappointment.

Our Melbourne performances were in the cosy little St Martin's Theatre, once home to Australia's oldest troupe, the Melbourne Theatre Company under the management (for his second spell in charge) of one of the biggest names in Australian theatre, John Sumner. John had directed the world premiere of *the most historically significant play in Australia's theatre history*, Ray Lawler's *Summer of the Seventeenth Doll*. He led the move to have the street in which the St Martin's Theatre stood renamed as St Martin's Lane. There was considerable local opposition (*lane suggests a narrow winding country road*) until he pointed out that St Martin's Lane was one of the most important streets in London housing some of the most famous theatres in the world - and the name change was agreed. Thanks to John we had enthusiastic audiences, and a really satisfying time in his city. We were shown the building site which was to become the Melbourne Arts Centre, the hub of future world-class International Arts Festivals. I haven't appeared at one yet, but if anyone in Melbourne is reading this . . . .

Our Manager for this section of the tour, Cliff Hocking, was also manager for Barry Humphries. Barry played Mr Sowerby, the undertaker, in the first (1960) London production of *Oliver*, and was by then back home, touring Australia with his solo revue. We arrived in Perth to discover Barry already ensconced in the massive 2,500-seat His Majesty's Theatre, while we made our way to the more sedate 700-seat Playhouse. I had worked with Barry in a Joan Littlewood production of Frank Norman's play *Kayf Up West* at Stratford East in 1964, so it was great to meet up with him again - and to see his latest show. It included his trademark Melbourne housewife Mrs Norm Everage alongside some newer, contrasting characters: it would be another two years before plain Mrs Everage metamorphosed into the glamorous, gladioli-waving Superstar, Dame Edna.

Perth is an attractive city, and the schedule allowed us time to enjoy the coast. We had left London as spring was breaking, and arrived in Australia at the start of their winter, so the sunnier weather on the west coast was most welcome. I've always remembered 1968 as the year of three winters. Adelaide was particularly chilly: the winds seemed to arrive direct from the Antarctic and blew straight up the wide streets of a very modern city which reminded me a little of Plymouth. Not until our final date, Darwin, did I really feel warm, and by then we had played the Federal Capital, Canberra as well as Bathurst and Newcastle.

In Sydney I had been invited to a working men's club: nothing like the working men's clubs I was used to in the Nottinghamshire mining villages which were usually little more than a dartboard, a bar, and a tiny stage with a 'slash' back-drop. In Sydney a working-man's club is more likely to be a huge town centre block five storeys high. Four storeys of bars, with a swimming pool on the top floor. Not many 'working men' in the swimming pool on the evening of my visit, but the bars were all extremely busy.

In the border city of Mildura we performed in a charming little arts centre; an attractive new building set in a park high above the Murray River with a picturesque view over acres of vineyards on the far bank. The next morning I said to a guy in the town that I thought Mildura had the nicest little theatre we'd seen anywhere in Australia. "Have we got a theatre?" he said. "I didn't know we had a theatre. We do have the longest bar in the world. It's in the Guinness Book of Records". He took me to see it.

A long, boring room - not quite sawdust on the floor, but close - and a horse-shoe shaped bar which started at the end wall, ran almost to the far end, then curved round and continued back to the starting wall. I had a great time out there, met some fantastic people and have only happy memories - but it doesn't stop me occasionally remembering Australia as "the longest bar in the world".

Chapter Seventeen: GBS: From Max to Brian.

Max Adrian was an actor: the only way he could play Shaw was to 'get into character'. Full costume and make-up. In fact, three full costumes, and three changes of make-up including wigs, beards moustaches and eye-brows. The script (by Michael Voysey) had him as a young man in Act One, progressing to the ninety-year-old by Act Three. Max was 64 at the time of our Australian tour, so this was quite a formidable challenge, both on stage and off.

No time to put his feet up in the intervals: he had to strip down to his underpants, rip off all the false hair, and start all over again. However, this thrice-nightly application and cleaning-off of spirit gum developed a skin rash which was both painful and unsightly. Max put the blame on the Australian spirit gum. Why it should be any different to the

British gum I couldn't imagine but, to be fair, he had been doing the show regularly at home without suffering any difficulties so I faxed the British Council in London and got them to air-mail out a large bottle of the home-grown variety. By the time it arrived the rash had already started to clear up, but we had made an effort, demonstrated our concern, gone to some trouble - all the things that are expected of one when touring with an actor.

I am not an actor. On those few occasions when I have been forced to tread the boards, it was either as an emergency understudy or, as actually happened on a couple of occasions, I had written such a lengthy part for the lead character in one of my own scripts that no-one else would learn it just for one or two nights at a Festival. My appearances were the result of necessity rather than desire. Getting 'into character', wearing costumes and make-up was not for me. The Scottish Community Drama Association organised an annual One Act Play Festival, and one year we entered my stage adaptation of Roni Robinson's moving radio play *Last Loves*, set in a care home. In the radio version the lead had been played by Richard Wilson, but his character was hardly ever off stage and no-one else was prepared to learn the part just for the one night. He was supposed to be 70, roughly my age at the time, so I gave it a go. The play was well reviewed - *"warmly crafted, and laced with affectionate gentle humour"* - but I'm not sure I would want to do it again.

Speaking to societies is something else. I can be myself, talking about my own experiences. No pretence. This is me: this is what I do. I had returned home after a year in the Middle East to work, first, as Administrator of the MacRobert Arts Centre in Stirling, and then Director of Kirkcaldy's Adam Smith Theatre. Societies are always seeking speakers for their monthly meetings, and in both towns I was invited to promote our current theatre programme. I would pad this out with anecdotes from my overseas experiences touring with

British Council dance and drama companies, usually under the title *Around The World In Eighty Plays*. Later, I added a second theatre talk, *The View From The Wings*: a sideways look at theatrical disasters from the stage manager's point of view. However, there are plenty of people doing theatre anecdotes: I wanted to move up a grade, and develop a talk with more serious content. Not necessarily a serious talk - any play or presentation needs a degree of humour - but something based in the real world rather than the artificial world of the theatre. My eight tours of the Indian sub-continent had interested me in the history of British India and encouraged me to write a theatre script *Letters From The Hen House* detailing the lives of British women in India during the 120 years prior to Independence. The play was written, in part, as a response to critics who hinted I didn't write many good female roles: it has six excellent parts for the ladies, and only four men. It was staged at the Byre Theatre in St Andrews in 2006 at fairly short notice: they had a cancellation, and offered me the dates. We went on in late June (not a good time for drama) and did over 50% business, covering our costs.

I used parts of that script together with some of my research material to put together a talk *Women of the Raj*. Sita Ram Pande, a former sepoy in the Indian army, wrote *"the Englishwoman in India has, during the last thirty years, been the cause of half the bitter feelings between the races. It was their presence at Cawnpore and Lucknow that pointed the sword of revenge after the Mutiny, and it is their constantly increasing influence now that widens the gulf of ill-feeling"* and I discovered considerable support for this argument in the letters and diaries of the time. An Englishman, John Morris, had written *"Most of them, the British memsahibs, may have started out as perfectly reasonable, decent girls, but they developed into what I can only describe as the most awful old harridans. I think they were very largely responsible for the break-down in relations between the British and the Indians"*.

Later arrivals fitted in much better, and there was a genuine feeling of sadness when Independence eventually forced them all to return to Britain, facing *"the final indignity of carrying their own bags and cases to the second and third class railway carriages"*. *Women of the Raj* tells their stories and has proved particularly successful at Ladies Lunches, and with the Women's Institutes and U3As.

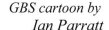
GBS cartoon by
Ian Parratt

Looking for another worldly subject I kept returning to George Bernard Shaw. I had worked on plays by him, and about him; I had worked with people who knew him (including Max Adrian); I had worked with two stars - Sir John Gielgud and Dame Sybil Thorndike, who had actually been directed by him. He had also shared responsibility with Peter O'Toole for my own choice of career - a career which, incidentally, would actually provide an opportunity to work with Mr O'Toole, but we'll save that particular 'experience' for a later chapter.

Obviously there would be no costumes, no false hair, no 'getting into character'. This talk would be by me, and about what I had learned of Shaw from his plays, his politics, his music, his love life, and from personal memories of people who had known him and worked with him. Shaw, the man. Shaw, the very humorous man. Shaw who admitted that he was *"occasionally vulgar, but it seemed to me that didn't matter very much so long as you made people laugh.*

I was merely playing the clown" he added "and *the clown is often the best part of the circus"*. The talk became a 'solo performance', *GBS: Playing The Clown*, and it may just be the best thing that I shall ever do. It has already been booked in London, Belfast, France and Scotland, but is equally popular with local societies such as the English-Speaking Union, the University of the Third Age and National Trust venues and Associations.

I had intended it for the Literary Festival circuit, and sent out the usual three hundred letters and e-mails. Received the usual twenty responses: "*fully booked for this season, but maybe next year*". Yeah, right. As part of that process I had signed up to receive email newsletters from many of the Festivals, and suddenly received one from Penzance asking me what I would like to see in next year's Festival. "*I'd like to see my solo presentation about the life, loves and writings of George Bernard Shaw*". Within 36 hours I had a response from the Festival Director, Peter Levin: "*Yes, OK*", and that was the closest we got to a contract. Peter phoned to tell me what he could afford in the way of 'expenses': I wasn't in a position to argue. I had a most enjoyable couple of days in Penzance: did my (beautifully-staged) presentation in the Acorn Theatre, met a few of my fellow participants, and saw some of the other events - notably Peter Gale's impressive production of *Noye's Fludde* in St Mary's Church (yes really, that Peter Gale - the author, Cornwall resident, and very accomplished musician). A really happy little Festival in a very friendly town. The publicity engendered in the West Country from that one performance has taken me back regularly to the region, mainly to the U3As and theatres, but including two more excellent local Festivals in Dawlish and Launceston. Terrific audiences everywhere.

The premise of *Playing The Clown* is quite simple: I introduce myself - I am Brian, not Bernard - and explain that I am here to give a talk about the man often described as the best playwright since Shakespeare. Only then do I go behind the lectern, put on my glasses, and start the lecture. I have barely begun before Shaw breaks away stage left and turns the lecture into a dialogue, correcting me, adding personal details to my bare facts, finishing my sentences. The intention was that the lecturer would have centre stage, with interruptions from the playwright - and that was how it worked until Belfast. I was performing in the magnificent Linen Hall Library to a very knowledgeable audience, but on a tiny platform - and in lighting which had obviously been focussed on a previous artiste working at floor level, since all the spotlights were aimed at crotch-height. I had to work towards the front of this narrow rostrum, and with knees slightly bent so that my face could be seen. A generous response from a very friendly audience at the end - one of the reviews said "*I now feel I know the real GBS*" - but it had all been rather restricted. A few days later I was in a church hall in Minehead for the West Somerset National Trust Association, working on a flat floor with plenty of space between lectern and the front row, and this lack of restriction suddenly released Mr Shaw. He rushed around, chatting directly to the audience, and totally dominating the evening. That's the way it's been ever since, and I do so enjoy doing it. As long as I can still drive to venues and stay on my feet for an hour or so, I hope that *Playing The Clown* will continue to supplement my pension for a few more years.

Chapter Eighteen: From Billy Cotton to Donizetti.

Bernard Shaw wrote "Music is an essential part of my life". He had a decent baritone voice; he taught himself to sight-read a score and to play piano. He became a respected music critic, so respected that W H Auden described him as "possibly the greatest music critic who ever lived".

Playing The Clown, my solo performance about Shaw has proved so popular that I have added a second show, *Shaw On Music*. I am, however, the first to confess my own complete failure as a musician. Sidney Smith, the choirmaster at St Marks Church as well as music master at my Grammar School, threw me out of the choir when my voice broke and begged me to end my piano lessons with him. Despite these minor failings I can still claim, like Shaw, that music has been an essential part of my life.

Certainly there was little music in my boyhood home: we had no gramophone in the house although there was a pianola - with perhaps a dozen paper rolls. There was also a valve radio which alternated between the BBC Home and Light programmes, and Sundays brought us The Billy Cotton Band Show along with Max Jaffa and his Palm Court Orchestra. RAF colleagues introduced me to Tchaikovsky (his 4th Symphony), although my first LP purchase, made around that same time, was not classical but Frank Sinatra's *Songs for Swinging Lovers*. My first live concerts were neither classical nor pop, but the fantastic series of Jazz at the Philharmonic tours organised by Norman Granz and featuring Ella Fitzgerald, Louis Armstrong, Sarah Vaughan, Oscar Peterson, Roy Eldridge, Sonny Stitt, the Dave Brubeck Quartet, The Modern Jazz Quartet and the bands of Count Basie and Duke Ellington. We celebrated my 21st birthday in London at a John Dankworth Concert (with Dudley Moore on piano). By then I had started work, so was unable to attend what proved to be Nat King Cole's last London appearance.

My knowledge and interest in classical music developed considerably during my several tours with Sadler's Wells Royal Ballet. Their repertoire at that time included some contemporary works alongside the traditional ballet scores, and I was introduced to Shostakovich's Second Piano Concerto and Sir Arthur Bliss's score for *Checkmate*. Also to Boieldieu's Harp Concerto (written in 1800, but new to me).

It was at the famous first night of the MacMillan's *Romeo and Juliet* with Margot Fonteyn and Rudolf Nureyev at Covent Garden that I discovered Prokofiev - who would eventually lead me on to the delights of Stravinsky's *Firebird* and *Rites of Spring*. Touring with Sadlers Wells Royal Ballet was probably the most enjoyable period of what I laughingly call 'my career'. An extremely happy, hard-working company with a small, companionable, efficient technical crew. Our props man liked a drink or ten and got lost one night going home from the pub in Stratford-on-Avon. He asked directions of a policeman. "Just carry on crawling in that direction, sir. You'll find the hotel further up, on your left". On one of those Stratford evenings our final ballet was *The Dream*, Ashton's reworking of Shakespeare's *A Midsummer Night's Dream*. It had an attractive, atmospheric set, a beautifully lit woodland setting. After curtain down I was standing on top of Titania's bower clearing foliage when a local stage hand decided to dismantle the bower from underneath. As I scrambled from the debris of wood and leaves I remonstrated with him in a language any stage hand might understand (I seem to recall "blithering idiot" or words to that effect) and hinted that he might want to look for another job as there was clearly no place for him in the theatre. He eventually found another job: that blithering idiot went on to be Technical Director at Glyndebourne Opera House.

Having the word 'Royal' in the title meant that we were occasionally subject to some disruption during 'The Troubles'. One night we were half-way through the second ballet of a Triple Bill (Christopher Bruce's *Unfamiliar Playground*) at the Manchester Opera House when a bomb scare forced us to clear the theatre. There was just time for the dancers to grab coats before we were turned out into a typical Manchester evening - chilly and drizzling rain. Eventually the dancers took refuge in the pub where they found the orchestra already into their third round. When we finally got clearance from the police - after some forty-five minutes - we all reluctantly left the pub, returned to the theatre, and prepared for the third and final ballet, the ever-popular *Pineapple Poll*. Most of the audience came back; many had also discovered Manchester's pubs so there was a warm, friendly atmosphere in the theatre. The audience applauded the dancers; the dancers applauded the audience at the end of the most relaxed, most enjoyable, most alcohol-fuelled performance of *Pineapple Poll* ever seen on any stage.

In my experience, ballet dancers are probably the most hardworking people in show business. First thing every morning they have to do 'class' to exercise the muscles and ligaments: if they don't do this 'warm-up they leave themselves open to career-threatening strains and injuries. Class is followed by rehearsals for the next new production or revival coming into the repertoire. A lettuce leaf for lunch (they are all terrified about putting on weight), and then rehearsals for that evening's programme. Perhaps a change of principal, or replacing an injured dancer. Perhaps repositioning the corps de ballet, for whatever reason: there are, for instance, more swans on the lake in Liverpool, where the Empire Theatre stage is enormous, than there are on the tiny stage at Wolverhampton. Another lettuce leaf, then back in for the evening performance. And what do they do for relaxation after all that? They go off to a disco and dance! Those four tours with Sadlers Wells Royal Ballet were among the happiest periods of my career. A close, friendly, happy group - now , of course, resident in the Midlands as Birmingham Royal Ballet.

I did two seasons during 1966/7 for Scottish Opera, with Alexander Gibson as Musical Director and the fabulous Scottish National Orchestra in the pit. Over-flowing from the pit, in fact, as several of the seventy-five musicians involved in the first two parts of Wagner's Ring Cycle had to be squeezed into the stage boxes. I had moved on by the time they produced the remaining parts of the Cycle, and it was some years before I discovered how the story ended. The revivals and new productions during these two seasons also included two Verdi operas, *Otello* and *Falstaff*; Benjamin Britten's *Albert Herring*; Mozart's *Cosi fan Tutte*; Puccini's *La Boheme* and Gounod's *Faust*, all adding to my musical experience.

One lunchtime their Lighting Designer, Charles Bristow, on loan from Sadler's Wells, asked me to meet him in the office (the pub next door) where he explained that he had been unexpectedly summoned back to London. Would I do the lighting for *Faust* and *Otello*?
"I've cleared it with the management, if you're agreeable".
"When are you off?"
"Two o'clock train. Here are the plans".
I hadn't done much lighting since leaving the National Theatre, and suddenly found myself doing two operas which I had never seen, with the first one - *Faust* - dress rehearsing the following evening. With the help of directors and stage management we got by, but were all greatly relieved to see Charles back in time for the Wagner. However, I can now claim to have done the lighting for both Sir Laurence Olivier's *Othello* and Sir Charles Craig's *Otello*.

Peter Ebert (son and biographer of Glyndebourne's Carl Ebert) and Anthony Besch shared the directing chores at Scottish Opera, and at the end of my second season with them Mr Besch asked if I would light and stage manage a double bill of Poulenc operas at the Camden Festival in London. *La Voix Humaine*, and *Les Mamelles de Teresias*. I had some of Poulenc's chamber music on disc, in particular the Clarinet Sonata and the Sextet, but knew nothing about his operas so this would be a great chance to extend my musical knowledge. Musical Director was Roger Norrington (now Sir Roger) and anyone involved with opera will be aware that the MD has more-or-less total control of the Dress Rehearsal: his last chance to pull everything together for the First Night due to start in a few hours time. I have seen Sir Alexander Gibson give a withering look towards any director who attempted to interrupt him during a Scottish Opera dress rehearsal. At Camden, we had got through *La Voix Humaine* without any histrionics, but it might only take a little thing to disturb the peace. *Les Mamelles* (yes, it really does mean that) was in two scenes, with an intermezzo covering a scene change.

We were perhaps thirty seconds into the intermezzo when Mr Norrington stopped the orchestra to correct something: I quickly called everyone back on stage into their positions at the end of Scene One. Mr Norrington asked the orchestra to continue from the point where they had stopped and, with my fingers crossed behind my back *(please, please, please don't shout at me)* I went through the curtains, apologised, and said that they would have to go back to a point just before the intermezzo: I even gave him the bar number; 126. "Why?". "Because I have all the singers standing by for a costume change, and all the stage staff standing by for a scene change, and they need to know that they can do it within the length of the intermezzo. This is their only opportunity". A very long silence, and then "Well ladies and gentlemen, it seems we must go back to Bar 126". At the end of the run we shook hands and he said I was one of the best stage managers he had worked with, presumably because of that one moment. He was young: he will have worked with many better since.

Our Director at Stirling's MacRobert Centre, Roy McEwan, was one of the most musically-knowledgeable men I have ever worked with. His scheduled seasons with the BBC Scottish Symphony Orchestra introduced me to, and taught me to appreciate, a wide range of orchestral music. My CD collection has an even wider range as it includes a lot of stuff bought for use as incidental or scene change music in my various productions.

It was a show at the Saville Theatre which first aroused my interest in musical theatre. Bernstein's musical *Candide* opened at the Saville on April 30th 1959 with Denis Quilley in the title role. For someone like me, a newcomer to the business, it seemed to be the ultimate in theatrical entertainment, bringing together literature, singing, dancing, music, acting and design (the sets were by Osbert Lancaster, and lyrics by Sondheim).

By the time of my second Palladium pantomime I had switched jobs, and was working backstage. Star of *Humpty Dumpty* was the irrepressible Harry Secombe, a genuinely good guy. There are perhaps half-a-dozen artistes about whom no-one has a bad word, and Harry was on everyone's list. We would chat in the wings while he was waiting to go on, and one evening he showed me a letter he had just picked up at the stage door. He had agreed to do a Midnight Matinee for charity, and the letter was to say that he would be top of the bill. "Big deal" he said. "All that means is that I hang around chatting and drinking until about 3.00am, and then get on stage to find that everyone's yawning and looking at their watches". But he did it. He would tell the story of his young grandson watching him put on his dinner jacket and asking "why do you wear that suit, grandpa? You know you always have a headache in the morning".

His style was perfect for panto, but in *Humpty Dumpty* he went on and sang a Welsh folk song, David of the White Rock. In Welsh! Why? Well, my guess is that it was his latest recording: Lou Grade owned Associated Television, which owned the Palladium - and also owned Pye Records, for whom Harry recorded at that time. They probably hoped that by singing it in the pantomime they would sell more copies of the record. It was all wheels within wheels in the Lou Grade 'empire': he was also agent to most of the top stars and would take back 15% of their salaries when he booked his own artistes into his own theatres or television shows.

Anyway, a Welsh folk song in the middle of *Humpty Dumpty* seemed totally out of place to me, and I made a mental note that when, (not if), when I directed my first pantomime all of the songs and dances would be as relevant to the plotline as in any of the best musicals. It took a long time but in 1987 when I took over as director of the Adam Smith Theatre in Kirkcaldy I discovered that my contract committed me to 'write and direct the annual pantomime'. I was therefore delighted to read Mary Brennan's review in the Glasgow Herald: *"I was very much taken with the way director Brian Freeland and choreographer Jane Harrod make the various dance sequences fit in with the story. In other panto villages the streets are hoaching with grinning peasants. Here a chorus of merry milkmaids pursue a recalcitrant cow while in a later scene a group of the Giant's prisoners droop and pine in chains - this kind of inventiveness helps refresh traditions and makes Kirkcaldy's Jack and the Beanstalk a lively and entertaining show".*

I went on to write and direct the next two Kirkcaldy pantomimes. The first, *Humpty Dumpty*, had squeaky-voiced Londoner Joe Pasquale as a newly-hatched 'alien' in an otherwise all-Scottish cast, a cast which included Scotland's favourite magician John Shearer as King, and the popular folk/jazz singer Alastair McDonald as Dame. I had been watching Joe win through to the Final of the New Faces series on TV and I suspected that he would be perfect in the role, which he was. His engaging personality and willingness to tackle crazy bits of stage business endeared him to both cast and audience. An original talent and a hard-working guy; his huge success is well-deserved.

Alexander Selkirk, the original castaway on whom Daniel Defoe based his story of Robinson Crusoe, was born in the village of Lower Largo just a few miles to the north of Kirkcaldy. I thought it was time to bring that story 'home', so my third and final pantomime had its opening and closing scenes set in Lower Largo. Actor Micky McPherson, who had been an excellent foil to Joe Pasquale the previous Christmas, moved up to the title role as a cheeky *Robinson Crusoe*. Singing pianist Derek Barron played his brother 'Enrico Crusoe', the romantic lead (I don't apologise for that name: it still makes me laugh, although it is probably funnier if you are old enough to remember the opera singer Enrico Caruso). We had a terrific Fife-born Mrs Crusoe in the (not inconsiderable) figure of the late Nikki Young, and Derek Lord from STV's *Take The High Road* as a really hissable baddie, the Laird o' Lundy.

Alexander Selkirk had been put ashore in September 1704 on the island of Juan Fernandez following a disagreement with his captain over the seaworthiness of their ship (which did, indeed, founder - in sight of some Spanish sailors who took the surviving crew prisoners). Selkirk was alone on that island for four years and four months with only feral goats for company (no, there was no Man Friday). The goats provided him with meat, milk, and hides for clothing. I wanted to find some way to demonstrate this 'period of loneliness' and asked Tommy Chipperfield, the circus owner, if he had any trained goats we could hire. He smiled politely, in the way that people smile when dealing with an obvious simpleton, and explained gently that you cannot train goats. A dog, a horse or an elephant is capable of learning a complete routine, and would probably perform it perfectly even without the trainer in the ring, but goats do not have that ability. What they can do, what they love to do, is climb. Put a box or a barrel in front of them and they will jump on it. Put a plank across to another box and they will 'walk the plank'. He had goats, and used them occasionally in public shows : the trainer simply built up different levels of boxes and planks and encouraged the goats to do what they would have done anyway. This seemed perfect. Crusoe was on a desert island: driftwood and boxes could be logically scattered all over the stage. So it was all agreed. Chipperfield's trainer spent a day with Micky

MacPherson to show him the ropes, and then drove off. He had lost a winter's feed bill; we had gained three pygmy goats. They were quite unpredictable and caused the backstage staff a few headaches, but they proved the real stars of the show - twice daily.

Before I leave Kirkcaldy, one last 'musical' memory. My predecessor at the Adam Smith Theatre, Chris Potter, was extremely knowledgeable about musicals and had usually staged one himself early in the autumn season. My own seasons often included medium-scale touring musicals so it wasn't until the autumn of 1989 that I was able to fulfil a personal ambition with our own new production of the French show which had been a huge success in London and New York but had had only one previous Scottish airing - *Irma La Douce*. The show had opened in Paris, where it ran for four years, and had music by Marguerite Monnot who had written songs for Edith Piaf. Book and lyrics were by Alexandra Breffort, but these were rewritten (rather than translated) by Julian More, David Heneker and Monty Norman for the London production in 1958, directed by Peter Brook. Toe-tapping music, witty lyrics, colourful sets, strong characters: there can only be one reason why the amateur operatic societies don't add it to their far too limited repertoire - there is only one female in the cast, the title role, and most amateur societies have to find work for a (largely female) chorus, plus some juicy parts for the female principals.

Steven Wren as the student who falls in love with the prostitute Irma (Maria Miller) led a brilliant cast - all Scottish, except John Adam-Baker who would return as a unexpectedly intellectual Man Friday in *Robinson Crusoe*. Our brilliant musical arrangements were by yet another Scot, Robert Pettigrew and, with just a quintet instead of a full pit band, he still managed to capture the colourful Parisian underworld atmosphere. You may never get a chance to see a live performance of this wonderful little show, so allow me to recommend the Original Cast CDs of the London and Broadway productions. Mine both get played regularly, and help to remind me of a very happy show. Just one small regret: knowing of his deep interest in, and extensive knowledge of, musicals I genuinely wanted to hear Chris Potter's views on the production. Unfortunately he had an even stronger interest than musicals: he made it to the Adam Smith Theatre, but never got past the bar.

I had already been employed as professional director for a few amateur musical productions, including *Oh What a Lovely War* in Qatar and *Aladdin* in Bahrain as well as three Gilbert & Sullivan operettas for the Dunfermline G&S Society. The Kirkcaldy G&S Society invited me to direct their next production and I was about to make a gracious and humble acceptance when their spokesman went on to say "we saw your *Gondoliers* in Dunfermline. Didn't think much of it, but it's so difficult to find directors" and suddenly, sadly, I couldn't find space in my empty diary to fit them in.

I group amateur dramatic and operatic societies into three divisions. It is easy to spot a Division One society: without in any way damaging the integrity of the intentions of the original writer and composer, they stamp their own personality on a production with imaginative touches that give it a freshness and excitement not found in the lower divisions.

Division Two societies will only stage shows which they have seen elsewhere. If what they saw was a professional production, or even performed by a Division One company, then they might get away with it, but sometimes they merely end up producing a pale carbon copy of something which was itself already a pale carbon copy by a fellow Division Two group.

Division Three societies, happily a small minority, have selection committees who put forward shows which they have neither seen nor read. One society interviewed me as prospective director (they, of course, called it producer) for their intended production of *The Best Little Whorehouse in Texas* and asked "It will be alright to bring the children, won't it?" I suggested that the clue was probably in the title. "So long as you're happy to explain to them what goes on in a whorehouse, then there shouldn't be any problems".

Another society planned to stage *Chess*. Tim Rice wrote in the libretto that he didn't believe the original production team ever got it quite right despite their several attempts to turn a group of songs into an integrated musical. "Future directors should feel free to find their own way through the available material" he wrote. That really appealed to me and I agreed to give it a go - but it soon became clear that the society had only four men. Four good men: an asset to any society, but simply not enough. More will turn up at auditions, I was told, but they didn't. I explained that *Chess* was not possible with only four men: would they please arrange a committee meeting and let me know their intentions at the next rehearsal. They had their meeting; they agreed that *Chess* was not practical and they had chosen an alternative musical. Would I stay on and direct it? "That rather depends on what you have chosen". They, the selection committee of this company with only four men, had chosen - *Seven Brides for Seven Brothers*. No, I didn't do it.

My interview with the committee at Motherwell and Wishaw Amateur Operatic Society started badly; asked about my plans for *Brigadoon* I did my usual spiel about 'the integrity of the authors' intentions', and as illustration, suggested that for the sake of artistic credibility and given the present 'anti-paedophile' climate, we should not have a fifty-year-old Tommy wooing a twenty-year-old Fiona. There was a long, uncomfortable silence: only later did I discover that the fifty-year-old on the interviewing panel had already been pencilled in to play Tommy. In the event he carried off the part rather well. Very experienced and with an excellent singing voice, but with one major drawback - he wouldn't dance, and had to be 'hidden' in all the relevant dance routines. This was a great pity because Paula McGilvray's *"choreography had the whole stage swirling with movement during the numerous dance sequences"* according to the NODA review, which ended *"Altogether a show for which the production team can take much credit"*. Once they accepted that it wasn't going to be a 'carbon copy' production the company really pulled out all the stops, and I hope they were as proud of the end product as I was. First Division status, I thought.

Sometimes a director is forced to change the style or period of a production for reasons beyond his or her control. For three years from 2005 I had the (mostly) pleasure of directing Tayside Opera, an amateur grand opera company based in Dundee. I took over their production of *La Traviata* at very short notice when their contracted director had to move down to London, and at our single - very brief - meeting I really only had time to ask him about the chorus. " Can they all sing and dance?" I asked. "Oh, yes" he said, edging towards the door, "but not at the same time". And then he was off - looking, I thought, rather relieved.

I asked the company to run what they had rehearsed so far, and they did the opening of Act One when the visitors arrive at Violetta's salon: the music suggested a busy bustling entrance, but the singers crept in and hugged the rear wall of the set where they performed (as I said at the time) rather like singing wallpaper. Happily the music staff were getting a lovely sound from them, so my main task would be to get them thinking as individuals, as minor characters rather than a single amorphous 'lump' of chorus. For the first two years they performed in the intimate Gardyne Theatre at Dundee College, with its small but incredibly helpful and efficient technical crew. For some reason Tayside Opera worked without a stage manager, but the theatre's electrician, Phil

Cooney, was also a musician so I was able to mark up a copy of the score with all the technical cues and he ran the show from the lighting control. Unorthodox certainly but, thanks to Phil, it worked.

La Traviata was followed by another Verdi opera, *Ernani*. Seldom done, and with good reason. It's a long opera, running over three hours which would involve overtime payments for the orchestra. It requires four full-stage sets, four sets of costumes and two male choruses. Tayside Opera, like so many amateur groups, not only had a tight budget but found it difficult to recruit even one full male chorus. To save money I combined most of act three with a shortened act four: this enabled us to lose an interval, one complete stage set and one costume change - saving us both time and money. It was risky, but the changes worked better than I dared hope. I have never seen a production of *Ernani* other than the DVD of the bizarre La Scala version with Placido Domingo, but I still believe that we acquitted ourselves well. Gardyne Theatre staff Jim Taylor, Phil Cooney and Colin Lowson provided some atmospheric sets and lighting but, most importantly, the singers were beginning to think and act as individuals rather than a Gilbertian chorus, adding some much-needed veracity to a rather unconvincing plot.

For their next production Tayside Opera chose Donizetti's joyous romantic comedy *L'Elisir d'Amore*. I love it; it's such fun, and we had a superb cast - but we didn't have a venue: the Gardyne Theatre was closed for renovations. The only alternative was the University's Bonar Hall which had limited technical facilities, no technical staff, and a highly varnished stage floor which could not be covered or painted, and was certainly not going to suggest a Spanish vine-yard. We needed an indoor setting, ideally one which contained flowers and books - and could have a varnished floor. Somewhere like a hospital ward? A hospital in northern Italy, perhaps, towards the end of WW2 as the Allies were fighting their way north, allowing a wounded soldier to be carried into the ward on a stretcher under the supervision of his Italian officer (Belcore). In the original score Nemerino is a penniless workman in love with his employer, Adina, a wealthy vineyard owner. Our Adina became the hospital Matron; Nemorino the cleaner, and the class divide between them was immediately established, with Belcore lined up as a much more likely suitor for Adina. Dulcamara, usually a travelling salesman, became a black marketeer, selling under-the-counter drugs to the hospital management. It all fell into place perfectly. Don't just take my word for it. The Scottish NODA representative, Roger Buist, wrote *"When I first heard that Tayside Opera was presenting Grand Opera in the limited confines of the Bonar Hall I was full of misgivings but, believe me, thanks to Brian Freeland's ingenious stage set, and his impressive reworking of the opera, the evening was a complete success. I was totally mesmerized by all that was going on, and I enjoyed the many 'subtle' comedic production touches"*.

Sir Denis Forman, a former Deputy Chairman of the Royal Opera House and author of The Good Opera Guide, said he could never understand why opera choruses always rushed on together, sang a song, and then all rushed off together. When you set your opera in a hospital ward it makes much more sense: a bell rings, and the 'visitors' rush in and join the 'patients' at their various bedsides. Ring another bell - end of visiting time, and they all leave. I encouraged the 'visitors' to work out their relationships with the 'patients', and we had some lovely little scenes at the bedsides: one 'patient' even organised a card school. The reviews for both production and principals were satisfying but the one which pleased me the most said that the opera "didn't have a chorus, but a full cast of minor characters". An end to 'singing wallpaper' and, sadly, an end to directing amateur operatic societies. *L'Elisir d'Amore* proved to be my final production. My busy speaking programme now makes it impossible to commit to the societies' long rehearsal periods, but I do miss it. A lot of work, usually for little reward - but when you see the kind of development which we achieved in Dundee it can be extremely satisfying.

Chapter Nineteen: From Cognac to Smallhythe

I suppose that the best known town - and, indeed, the best known product - on the River Charente is Cognac. Three of the major producers, Hennessy, Martell and Otard, have premises on the riverside with Camus and Remy Martin nearby: all offer guided tours and tasting sessions.

I am making this return visit in 2015, the 500th anniversary of the accession of King Francois 1st (1494-1547) who just happened to have been born in Cognac - and the town takes every opportunity to remind you of that fact. He succeeded his Valois cousin Louis XII (who left no male heir) on 1st January 1515, and shortly afterwards travelled to Rome to meet the Pope. An elderly Leonardo da Vinci (for reasons that are not entirely clear to me) was living in the Vatican at that time. King Francois offered him the use of a manor house at Clos Lucé near his own home in the Chateau d'Amboise, plus a annual pension of 10,000 scudi. Da Vinci took with him his most famous painting, the *Mona Lisa* which eventually ended up in the Louvre. Aged 64, Leonardo da Vinci crossed the Alps on a mule, and took up residence at Clos Lucé in the autumn of 1516, remaining there until his death on 2nd May 1519.

"There has never been another man born in the world who knew as much as Leonardo, not so much about painting, sculpture and architecture, as that he was a very great philosopher".

He was buried in the Chapel of Saint-Hubert at Amboise, but as the king's First Painter, Engineer and Architect his influence is most obvious in the construction of the Chateau de Chambord, the largest chateau in the Loire Valley.

"Chambord is to architecture what the Mona Lisa is to painting" wrote d'Haussonville. "It's the major work of the Renaissance; a work of genius, a unique concentration of intelligence". This architectural masterpiece earned Francois the nickname Le Roi Batisseur, the Builder King.

Cognac has a huge statue of the mounted King Francois leading his troops against the Swiss at the Battle of Marigny soon after his accession. You'll find it in Place Francois 1er (where else would it be?). When I asked at the Tourist Office about the significance of that particular battle there were smiles all round: apparently of the many battles fought by King Francois, Marigny was his only success. He lost several battles with the Italians over his claims to the kingdom of Naples (lost by his cousin in 1504), and was actually taken prisoner at the final confrontation in Pavia (1525). In the Treaty of Madrid of 1526 he gave up his claims to Milan, Burgundy, Artois and Flanders, and was allowed to return to France. He also lost out - to Charles V - in the 1519 election for a new Holy Roman Emperor.

Following his release from prison, the widower Francois married Eleanor of Austria, the sister of Charles V. Nationally, he became a great patron of arts and culture, introduced Renaissance art to France and established French as the national language. He also found time to involve himself in the business affairs of his home town. He allowed Cognac to tax the distribution of salt: this arrived in bulk from the coast for redistribution up river as far as Montignac. Now he arranged for the empty *gabarres* to carry *eau-de-vie* back downstream to Rochefort prior to exportation to England, the Netherlands and Denmark. This developing trade saw an expansion in Cognac's population from 3,000 to 18,000. Today more than 21,000 people work to produce and market up to 130 million bottles a year, which are sold in more than 100 countries.

The king's birthplace, the 13th century Chateau des Valois, has been largely rebuilt and is now the headquarters of the Otard cognac company. His involvement in the *eau-de-vie* industry was noted by the town's Museum of Art which celebrated the 500th anniversary with an exhibition of old distillery posters using various depictions of the King's head to sell their products.

Publicity is important, whether you're selling brandy or theatre seats. During my Arts Administration Degree Course in 1973 we were reminded of the despondent theatre manager *"who knew that only 50% of his publicity worked, but didn't know which 50%"*. Good productions, great performances, even brilliant publicity will not always guarantee 'House Full' signs.

Many years after its London premiere with Mrs Patrick Campbell in the title role, there was a revival of Shaw's play *Pygmalion* at the Grand Theatre, Wolverhampton where they advertised it as "the brilliant comedy by Oscar Wilde". Shaw heard about this and wrote to the theatre "the license for the performance of my play did not authorise you to advertise it as the brilliant comedy by Oscar Wilde". The producer replied "I am disinclined to offer an apology as the show has played to approximately three times as much money as it did when I billed it as being written by you. This will result in your receiving larger royalties than would otherwise have been the case, so I cannot see what you are grumbling about". Postcard from Shaw: "My compliments. Please continue the attribution. I am not grumbling: I am rejoicing".

Even managements as qualified as Lord Lloyd Webber and Sir Cameron Mackintosh have had disappointments in recent months. I sent Mr Mackintosh (as he then was) a copy of the musical comedy I had put together in 'the house with two kittens'. In fact I sent out about thirty copies, all with stamped addressed envelopes. Only five were returned, one of them from Cameron with (to his credit) a personal letter explaining that he had never been much attracted to backstage musicals. That was seventeen years ago: In 2014 he staged *Barnum* at Chichester. Maybe I should re-submit my script? And then again, maybe not. It had seemed quite enjoyable at the time, but pastiches of old black-and-white movies have probably had their day. The plot was built around a small Hollywood studio's attempts to complete a film version of the Dick Whittington story despite hitting all kinds of unexpected problems along the way. Not quite a panto, not quite a musical, but possibly an alternative Christmas entertainment in a town which already has a traditional pantomime. Most of the characters were familiar - Bogart, Cagney, Laurel & Hardy, Ruby Keeler & Dick Powell - and the working title was *Casablanca Here I Come*. There are some good - even laugh-out-loud - moments, but it would probably have been beyond the aspirations of most amateur musical societies - and much too expensive to risk commercially. I'll leave a copy in the filing cabinet: perhaps in fifty years time someone will re-discover Brian Freeland's forgotten 'masterpiece'.

In the 1980s I was at an Edinburgh Fringe performance of a one-woman show by the experienced and talented American actress Arlene Sterne, portraying some of her famous predecessors such as Ellen Terry and Sarah Bernhardt. She had excellent reviews in both New York and Edinburgh, but when I went to see the show I was one of only three people in the audience. Shortly after curtain up the gentleman sitting near me asked "Is this Venue 42?" "Two doors along" I replied, and then I was one of only two - the other being an old lady in the front row nibbling on a sandwich. In the interval I had a chat with the sound/lighting operator and suggested that if it weren't for the old lady, Miss Sterne could have cancelled the second half and I should happily come again another evening. He explained that the old lady hadn't paid; she just came in every night to get out of the cold. The message was passed backstage; the second half was cancelled, and Arlene Sterne joined me for a most pleasant meal - the start of an occasional trans-Atlantic contact which we hoped would lead to a British tour, but without success. Arlene was very much in my thoughts, however, when I took my G B Shaw presentation *Playing The Clown* to Ellen Terry's private Barn Theatre at Smallhythe for the National Trust in June 2015. A very, very special evening.

Chapter Twenty: From Beijing to New York.

There was one later experience in my career that tied in neatly with my National Service days: I finally went into China, as a Stage Manager with London Festival Ballet - interpreting for the stage and lighting technicians, and even managing to run the prompt corner in Mandarin Chinese. We did a week in Beijing and a week in Shanghai.

China in 1975 was not the China of today, open to western ideas and capital: there was hardly a car to be seen on Beijing's wide streets although bicycles were eight abreast, and everyone, men and women, wore those loose blue boiler suits. When asked how loose these suits should be, Mao Zedong supposedly replied "Loose enough to make the sexes indistinguishable". We were followed everywhere by crowds who had not seen a westerner for several years. One elderly man surreptitiously practised his English on me, his first opportunity to do so for a decade or more. One memory of that trip still haunts me today and it was the small child who suddenly looked up and saw us - then ran, screaming, to her father, hugging his legs and barely daring to look at us over her shoulder - absolutely terrified by her first sight of Europeans; of we 'foreign devils'.

Impressarios Victor and Lilian Hochhauser had established their reputations by bringing some of the most illustrious Russian artists and ensembles to the west; it was in their London home, watching the news on television, that Rostropovich learnt the Soviets had taken away his passport. He would not return to Russia for 16 years. It was their friendship with Rostropovich that led, in 1974, to the Russians declaring the Hochhausers *personae non gratae*.

Stripped of their principal sources of business, they turned instead to China. They had already brought the Chinese Acrobats of Shanghai to Britain in 1973, and two years later they took London Festival Ballet to China – only the second western company to be allowed in following the Cultural Revolution (the first had been a French orchestra). Undoubtedly, the fact that Festival Ballet's director Dame Beryl Grey was already known in China (she had performed there in 1966 dancing with a Chinese partner) must have helped to open a few doors for the Hochhausers. Dame Beryl was an inspirational leader, dealing with both the political and cultural establishments as well as the press - and sharing the top table with the President of China at positively the biggest dinner I have ever attended. I occasionally caught up with Dame Beryl in recent years through her involvement as a very active Patron of the Sussex Opera and Ballet Society, and we sometimes talked about that tour. It was an important one both for Festival Ballet and for Anglo-Chinese cultural relations, but there were problems - some involving the orchestra. Although it was wonderful to have our own band in the pit, the extra costs did put the accounts into the red - and some of their instruments had to be left behind at Shanghai airport because the plane was over-loaded. They followed on a few days later.

The Hochhauser connection led to two further memorable contracts: stage managing one of Lilian's 'International Stars of the Ballet' seasons at the Royal Festival Hall, and touring in Britain with the Peking Opera Troupe from Shanghai.

A couple of years later, when I directed my first *Mikado*, I decided to make it as oriental as possible and used elements of Japanese culture - sumo wrestlers, Noh theatre characters, puppeteers on mobile stools, and a South Korean farmer's dance in the production. Tit Willow was done in the style of Peking Opera. We had some Japanese visitors at one of the performances, and they had recognised all of these references as well as the onstage signs written in traditional Chinese/Japanese characters.

With the Ballet at the Festival Hall we set everything up in the morning, focussed the lights, and rehearsed all afternoon - after which all of the Festival Hall staff knocked off having finished their shift for the day. We had an entirely different crew for the evening show, with absolutely no knowledge of what we had been rehearsing all afternoon. I talked to the Hall Manager who accepted that it was an illogical situation but his hands were tied: if he said or did anything which might upset the Festival Hall staff then every Council-owned venue in Greater London was liable to be closed down within minutes. We are talking about the late-seventies: I understand things have improved since then. I do hope so.

Touring, especially one-night-stands, is fairly exhausting: different cities, different airports, different theatres every few days, sometimes every day so, early in 1981, I accepted the offer of a year's residency as Administrator of the then-unfinished National Theatre of the Gulf State of Qatar. My tasks were to train staff and prepare programmes for the eventual opening. Theatre, of course, is quite un-Islamic: Qatari women were not allowed to appear on stage or on television: if actresses were required they were imported from Egypt or Kuwait where the rules were rather more relaxed. Audiences were almost entirely male: the only women would be diplomats' wives or foreign nurses from the hospital. They would sometimes stage what they called 'family matinees' when married women could attend with their husbands and children, but single men would not be admitted.

It was important to define the purpose of their new theatre: they wanted it to be the Sadler's Wells of the Gulf, attracting leading foreign companies to their 500-seat venue, and they specifically mentioned the Royal Ballet and the Royal Shakespeare Company. Money, as Football's World Cup has proved, would not be a problem, but censorship certainly would be. I explained that classical female ballet dancers had bare arms and legs, and that the male dancers wore revealing tights: the censor was horrified. "Oh, no. When they dance here they will have to wear proper clothes". And the Shakespeare? "They will have to send me a copy of the script so that I can remove anything from the text which I consider un-Islamic: then, when they arrive, they will perform the play for me so that I can remove any unsuitable stage business". Given these strictures, when my direct boss the Minister of Culture told me that he was to head a cultural delegation to Paris I asked him what they would be going to see - expecting him to say the National Opera or the Comedie Francaise. His reply? "We have already booked - for the Folies Bergere".

I did my best to line up programmes of both theatre and cinema, but opening dates came and went and the building still wasn't completed. Most international visiting companies would be coming on their way to or from Europe: specific dates were important to them, but because of the delays in building completion we simply couldn't confirm dates. Some companies were more flexible, and I was delighted that the Turkish National Dance Company did eventually perform there with, I'm told, great success. I had long negotiations with the Turkish Ambassador who, of course, fully appreciated the censorship problems.

I visited both Damascus and Beirut to talk to other Muslim drama and dance companies, and to deal with the regional film distributor who would be providing films for us in Arabic or with Arabic sub-titles. Damascus was a beautiful city (I hope it still is but times have changed). My contacts there took me to a theatre show, and the Aleppo football team (staying in the same hotel) arranged a stand seat for me at their league match against Damascus and gave me a lift to the stadium in their team bus. It's sad to think about what has been happening in their country since then. Going back to Beirut was quite weird. My last time in that city centre had been for the interview with the night club owner, years before the Seven Day War. Now, after my meeting with the film distributors, I had to get a taxi through the 'green line' check point for my appointment with Abdel-Halim Caracalla, director of the Caracalla contemporary dance company. Caracalla's choreography fused eastern and western styles in a manner which was likely to push the boundaries of what might be acceptable in Qatar, but Abdel-Halim was confident that they could put together a programme that would satisfy our censor. On the way back into the city centre the taxi turned into a street, about 100 metres long, sloping uphill. The entire length of the street, and half of its width, was totally filled with bombed, burnt and damaged military vehicles stacked two or three high. Life in Beirut was slowly getting back to normal; hotels, shops and restaurants were busy again. Plenty of traffic on the streets. I didn't have time to visit the Casino which was some miles out of the City but even that, apparently, was back in business. Those piled up tanks and armoured vehicles, and the long lines of snipers' bullet-holes down almost every street corner building were clear evidence of the bad times not long past: something to ponder on as I flew back to Qatar.

The architect's plans for their 'National Theatre of Qatar' were developed from the designs for an existing British provincial repertory theatre: there's nothing wrong with that - Victorian specialist theatre architects such as J C Phipps often re-used sections of their designs. Unfortunately, in order to fit a Royal Box into the rear wall the architects had raised the roof at least five or six metres - and neglected to re-align the lighting bars making the lighting angles difficult, and one of the bars totally useless as its spotlights only hit the top of the proscenium arch. Had they done a little more research they would have understood that their Royal Box would not be used as such: Gulf Arab leaders do not sit behind their compatriots. Whenever Royalty was expected the front two rows of seats in the auditorium would be replaced with comfortable sofas and armchairs for the official guests, whose staff would keep them well supplied with black coffee and

Quality Street chocolates throughout the show. The Royal Box - its private bathroom complete with gold-plated taps - would eventually house TV cameras and their operators.

Removing the front two rows would not be difficult: the Lebanese builders had used only a thin covering of sandy concrete for the auditorium floor. Their attempts to fix the seating involved drilling holes which were too big for the bolts, filling the holes with glue and then sticking the bolts into the holes. At least thirty per cent of the seats were wobbling even before anyone had sat in them. We had a snag list several pages long, with safety on the fly floor being a major problem, but could not get the builders back to finish the work. There had been a fire towards the end of construction: they had not been insured, and making good the damage used up their remaining funds. Eventually Ove Arup were brought in to finish the building, but by then my year was nearly up and I was happy to get away. I cashed in my return ticket to London, bought a round-the-world ticket in the opposite direction with the intention of visiting as many friends as possible on the way home.

And catching up on theatre; uncensored theatre; live theatre - and the most wonderful thing about live theatre is that it is unpredictable: you really do not know what might happen next. I was present at the a matinee of *Barnum* in San Francisco on Saturday 24th January 1982. Jim Dale and Glenn Close were the stars in an excellent production, but it was an odd audience: either we had a very high proportion of hearing-impaired people, or perhaps there were a lot of foreigners listening to instantaneous translation?

Then the penny dropped: it was the afternoon of the Super Bowl Final. The local team, the San Francisco 49ers were playing the Cincinatti Bengals, and at least half of the audience were watching the live show in the theatre and listening to their pocket radios at the same time.

Inevitably, the final whistle blew at a quiet moment in the show - Barnum's duet with Jenny Lind. The 49ers had beaten the Bengals 26-21 and the audience went wild. They stood and cheered; the band stopped playing and they also stood and cheered (they probably had a TV set in the pit). Jim Dale told the audience "Ladies and Gentlemen, you are watching the collapse of a once-great musical". Twice he tried to get the show re-started, but as soon as the band began to play the audience cheered again. Only on his third attempt did the show continue. Live theatre: there's nothing like it. I saw Jim's solo show *Still Carrying On* when he was in London in 2015, and was reminded of Elaine Stritch's one-woman-show *At Liberty*: two lovable, talented entertainers offering very personal memories of their varied and fascinating careers in thoroughly professional performances.

In San Francisco I had seen the then-newly-released film *On Golden Pond* and a couple of weeks later told a New York taxi driver that I thought the two stars, Fonda and Hepburn, were certain to win the Oscars. "Oh, you bloody limeys, you think you know it all when it comes to acting: let's just wait and see, eh?" I hope he remembered me when the two did, indeed, win Oscars for Best Actor and Best Actress.

In Washington I stayed with America's cultural representative in Qatar and his wife, recently returned home from Doha. I visited the Smithsonian, saw the White House, and later enjoyed an excellent production of Terence Rattigan's play *The Browning Version.* In Washington you expect integrated casting and the Gilberts were played by an Afro-American couple: after an initial shock - after all, we didn't have black teachers at public schools in those times - I sat back and enjoyed the play. I felt less comfortable at a more recent British production of King Lear, with Derek Jacobi in the title role. The 'colour-blind casting' gave Lear two white daughters and one black, and I did find that distracting in a play which has illegitimacy as a key sub-plot.

I saw several shows in New York including *Forty-Second Street* with two British stars - Millicent Martin and Steve Arlen. Steve had been principal singer in the Casino-du-Liban night club show, and had endured his own stormy relationship with the insufferable Charley Henchis. As he took his solo bow at the end of *Forty-Second Street* the rest of the cast applauded him, and I realised that it was his first night in the role of the Producer. I went backstage to congratulate him: neither he nor his lady friend had planned any kind of celebration so we went for a meal and chatted about Beirut. Lacking dolls and pins we stuck forks into a Charley Henchis serviette.

Chapter Twenty-One: From Saintes to Nottingham.

Throughout this return trip to the Charente I have been impressed with the cleanliness of the towns and cities, and Saintes, second largest city on the river, was no exception. The extensive shopping lanes of the *Centre Ancien* around the impressive *Cathedrale St-Pierre* had pale stonework absolutely gleaming in the afternoon sunshine, with attractive displays in the windows of the myriad boutiques. I had arrived in late afternoon knowing that my hotel was on the far side of the city, but found the bridge closed, and police diverting traffic. There were huge crowds shouting and waving balloons and, having been a regular visitor to Paris over the years, I assumed that it was a demonstration against something or other. But no, this was Saintes, not Paris, and it was the weekend of the Saintes Triathlon: roads to the east of the bridge were closed for the competitors who would finish their cycling circuit just by the Roman *arc-de-Germanicus*, park their bikes on the numbered racks, and immediately set off on a running circuit - some of them barefoot - which would eventually bring them back to the arch and the finishing point.

It is entirely natural that the Roman arch should be the focal point of the event, and indeed of the city. Under its Latin name *Mediolanum Santonum*, Saintes had been the capital of the Roman province *Gallia Aquitania,* an area covering most of south-west France. There was, there is, very little industry in the area: both the Roman provincial capital and the modern city developed mainly as administrative centres. The old Roman settlement was on the west side of the bridge which carried the Agrippan Way, their main Lyon to Aquitaine road, across the River Charente. The huge double *Germanicus* arch, built in 18-19AD, was originally on that bank of the river, separating the traffic entering and leaving the capital. Having driven on the wrong side of the road for the previous two weeks I found myself wondering whether this very early, and extravagant, system of traffic control had carts entering by the left or right arch.

One of the twin arcs-de-Germanicus, and the Amphitheatre

That old Roman bridge was demolished in 1843 but not replaced until 1879 when the present *Pont Bernard-Palissy* was opened, and the *arc-de-Germanicus* moved to its current position. I am told that many of the main roads in present-day France still follow the routes of their Roman predecessors. The Roman origins are still very much in evidence in Saintes.

As well as the arch you can find parts of the thermal baths and the aqueduct and, in a high valley to the west of the city, the largest Roman amphitheatre outside of Italy. Built in the first century AD it could seat 15,000 spectators - roughly the entire population of *Medeolanum Santorum* at that time.

I've never thrown Christians to the lions - well, not yet, anyway - but for a few summers in Nottingham I became involved with large-scale outdoor entertainment, starting locally with the management of the city's team in the BBC TV's It's A Knockout competition. Playing against Lincoln we led for most of the afternoon, but lost both the final game and the mini-marathon and were narrowly pipped at the post. I had moved to Nottingham to work at the Playhouse. Stuart Burge had just replaced John Neville as Director following a period of discontent over the manner of John's dismissal. Stuart was the perfect choice in this situation: an excellent director with good contacts and, given his superb temperament, he was unlikely to upset anyone. He didn't rush into decisions, though. There would be an "er .. er .." or three before any answer, but I soon learned that in that pause he had worked out all the possible alternative answers and invariably selected the right one. He had wide experience in films and television where any directorial decision has to consider camera angles, running time, lighting, costume and set changes - and a wrong answer could cost time and money.

The playwright Peter Barnes, author of *The Ruling* Class, wrote of Stuart "*He looked like a bemused gnome who had turned vagueness into a higher art form.* Certainly Stuart believed that "*every decision made on any production must stem from the text - whether a classic or a new play*"; an attitude which I encompass whole-heartedly. How you tell the story is up to you but it is the author's story and you must respect that, although I had some sympathy for John Dexter when he reprimanded Arnold Wesker "Shut up, Arnold, or I'll direct this play the way you've written it".

I once attended a rather confusing lecture by Peter Barnes when he suggested - I'm sure I got this right - that playwrights were the only people able to direct their own plays because only they knew the author's intentions. So no more Shakespeare productions, then; or Shaw. No more Greek tragedy. Indeed, since July 2004, no more Peter Barnes. I suspect that he had been unhappy with the way certain directors had treated his own scripts, but he did end the lecture with a soaring endorsement of Stuart's direction of *The Ruling Class* at Nottingham. "*He admired actors and respected good scripts, and he did his job, wonderfully transforming craft into art. In a floating world he was the real thing*". Stuart's production not only introduced a major new playwright, but also a major new set designer in John Napier and, according to The Independent, cast actor Derek Godfrey in "the performance of his career" as the Earl of Gurney.

Stuart started as an actor himself (alongside Edith Evans) in a pre-war Michel Saint-Denis production, *The Witch of Edmonton*. Irving Wardle reports that he auditioned for George Devine's Young Vic company by reciting 'You are old, Father William' while standing on his head. His Young Vic experiences helped him formulate a 'golden rule': "*the need to bend a performance to accommodate audience response, and particularly so when working with younger audiences. It was necessary*", he felt, "*to create a tight structure within which the actors should be capable of improvising*" and I've found that 'rule' extremely helpful in my solo performances.

His Nottingham contract acknowledged that Stuart had on-going film and TV commitments, and that there would be guest directors - notably Jonathan Miller, Michael Blakemore and William Chappell. The Playhouse would also be working in repertoire, with two or three changes of play every week - and of course the guest directors would disappear after the first or second night. Someone had to be recruited to a new post of Repertoire Manager to maintain the standards - both artistic and technical - of all productions in the repertoire. That someone was me.

Stuart had directed the premiere of Christopher Fry's play *Curtmantle* during my time with the RSC, and I knew his General Manager George Rowbottom from our time together at the National (at the Old Vic). The repertoire they had scheduled at Nottingham was an extraordinary one for a provincial playhouse: It included *The Alchemist* (Jonson)*; Widower's Houses* (Shaw); *Playboy of the Western World* (Singe); *The Entertainer* (Osborne); Brecht's *Arturo Ui*, Shakespeare's *Macbeth*, a rarely-performed Farquhar *Love and a Bottle*, and two world premieres - *The Ruling Class* and Christopher Fry's *A Yard of Sun*.

Jonathan Miller's production of *A School For Scandal* had just opened when I arrived. He would later add an interesting *Seagull* (Chekhov), and an impressive *King Lear* with a superb Michael Hordern in the title role. *Lear* rehearsals were fascinating since our director was, of course, a fully-qualified doctor, able to diagnose the exact medical condition of the failing king from the symptoms provided within Shakespeare's text. I don't think Michael Hordern was ever totally sure of his lines in the mad scene: he patrolled back and forth along the front of the stage, rather like a caged lion in a zoo, enabling him to be near the stage manager's desk should he need a prompt. Indeed, one night, he exited right and checked the prompt script before returning to continue the scene.

Michael met and married his wife Eveline when they were both in the Little Theatre company at Bristol some ten years before my spell in that same city, but I had worked with him briefly at the RSC when he coped wonderfully with Ulysses great speech in *Troilus and Cressida* - without any obvious prompts, so far as I could tell. He had an even longer speech, lasting thirteen minutes, at the beginning of Tom Stoppard's play *Jumpers* (1972), remembered by Adam Benedick in The Independent. "*Who could forget the sight of Hordern's anguished moral philosopher weaving one intricate fancy after another into a web of almost comic absurdity? What gave Hordern's acting its zest and spontaneity was probably nerves. Uncertain and insecure, he made much of the text sound as if he was indeed hammering it out for himself. Whether he was or wasn't, he made it seem so*".

Sir Michael (as he had deservedly become) died in 1995: perhaps three or four years earlier he had spied me from the other side of Oxford Street and wove his way through the heavy traffic just to say hello. What a lovely man. How I wish I had seen his doddery waiter in the 1990 production of Bernard Shaw's play *You Never Can Tell*. That sounds like the ideal casting.

Stuart had programmed John Osborne's musical play *The Entertainer* for this 1969 season but hadn't been able to cast the lead role. With time running out he asked for suggestions, and I recalled that Denis Quilley was about to return from Australia and would be looking for work. Stuart remembered him as a skinny young singing actor from the *Candide/Airs on a Shoestring/Grab Me a Gondola* days, but I was able to confirm that he had filled out and matured. We practically met him at the airport: he was offered the role, accepted, and came up and joined the company.

Ex-dancer/designer William Chappell directed *The Entertainer*. Denis, absolutely perfect as Archie Rice, was next cast alongside Leonard Rossiter's Hitler-character in Michael Blakemore's production of Brecht's *Arturo Ui*. Michael saw a performance of *The Entertainer* and told Denis that he ought to be at the National Theatre. "By God, I'd love that" said Denis. Blakemore passed this on to Olivier and, within months they were both there. Michael Blakemore as Associate Director, and Denis playing a wide range of leading roles - including co-starring with Olivier in *Long Day's Journey Into Night*. He worked regularly at the National throughout the rest of his life: "*there was a vacant slot for a man of my age and weight in the upper-middle of the company, and I just happened to fit it*".

He also starred in two major musicals, *Sweeney Todd* and *La Cage aux Folles*. I'm happy to think that I might have played a very tiny part in the success story of this friendly, talented, hard-working guy. In that same season I engaged a young, Leicester-born drama student as Acting ASM. His name was Michael Kitchen: I wonder what happened to him?

Up until 1969 the Playhouse organised an annual two-week arts festival. The last of these included an afternoon poetry recital by an 86-year-old Dame Sybil Thorndike. This was quite a coup for the Playhouse, and we painted the dressing room, laid a new carpet, ordered flowers and arranged for a car to collect her from the station. My four stage hands had been recruited from the dole queue; young men caught up in the slump following the decline of the mining industry. They had never heard of Dame Sybil Thorndike, and couldn't understand why we were making all this fuss over some aging actress. They were at the side of the stage when she arrived, beer bottles in unwashed hands. She put down her bags, and immediately went across to them; shook their unwashed hands; asked their names (and remembered them); asked them about their families, about life in Nottingham, about the local industrial problems. The four lads stood spellbound in the wings throughout the recital and, at the end, were queuing outside her dressing room door, waiting to carry her bags and her flowers out to the car. They practically kissed her goodbye, and stood waving as the car pulled away.

Riddled with arthritis, Dame Sybil continued her voice exercises and piano studies until she died in her 94th year. Committed socialist; committed Christian. Tiny in stature, but a great, great lady, and we were thrilled to have had the honour and pleasure of her company that afternoon.

In 1970 the Council decided to mount a larger City-wide Festival, using more venues, and with outdoor events in Wollaton Park, in the Old Market Square and along the River Trent. They engaged an expert in the field, Mr Richard Gregson-Williams, previously involved with the Exeter and York Festivals, and I joined his team. Hopes were high. "The biggest, most stupendous" wrote the Nottingham Post. "we will rival Edinburgh". The Council budgeted £25,000. Richard Gregson-Williams wasn't strong on accounting: officers from the City Treasurer's Department sat him down one day and explained that his planned programme was running way over-budget: some events would have to be scaled back or omitted altogether. Two hours later they had agreed on a series of cutbacks sufficient to balance the books. "So how much have we saved?" asked Richard. "£7,500" he was told. "Oh, that's perfect. Now I can afford to book Marlene Dietrich for a concert in the Playhouse". Clearly trained in the George Osborne School of Accountancy.

He was basically a 'music' man, I think, like so many Festival Directors, and I found that I was increasingly involved in the management and organisation of the 'popular', outdoor events such as The Festival in the Square. This operated on the Old Market Square, with the city's impressive Council House at the top end. There are two enormous stone lions in front of the Council House which, according to local legend, roar whenever a virgin passes. The programme included live entertainment at lunchtimes and 'going-home' time and, with only limited income from concessionaires, this had to operate on a tight budget. We engaged a mixture of amateur and professional performers. Temple's Agency, which booked acts for carnivals and arena events, was based in the city (they are now in Melton Mowbray) and Miss Temple found us an 'attention grabber' to catch the press and television. This was a sway-pole act, Leone and Tonya, a couple who did acrobatics on top of a very tall bendy pole. The only possible site for the pole was the flower bed above the ladies toilets, and the couple met the Council gardeners to check whether the soil was deep enough to hold their guy lines. It was. Only just, apparently, but thus encouraged we went ahead and booked them for the first weekend to attract maximum publicity for the remainder of the programme. The pictures of them swaying above the tops of passing buses appeared on television news, and in all the papers. Incidentally, the couple had two sway-poles: the other was in store in Australia, and they would spend British winters touring in the Antipodean summers.

Out at Wollaton Park, where we could charge for admission (and car parking) we mounted a huge balloon extravaganza, some show jumping, the last night fireworks, and a jousting tournament attended by Princess Margaret which attracted an audience of 50,000. Most of the riders were film stuntmen, and I realised that it might be a fun afternoon when I heard that one of these stuntmen had phoned his opponent to 'talk tactics' and was told "Tactics be damned: I'm going to knock thee off tha bloody 'orse".

The balloon race also proved quite exciting. The Lord Mayor Councillor Oscar Watkinson was scheduled to fly in the first balloon but couldn't be found and a radio journalist George Luce took his place. The balloon got caught in a thermal and a velcro seal was forced open: the pilot had to 'burn like mad' and managed to make an emergency landing in a small front garden with only a pint of fuel remaining. George Luce's commentary was later broadcast on Radio 4's *You and Yours* programme. Undaunted by all this, Councillor Watkinson went airborne the following day.

I had a lovely flat in The Park, a quiet Victorian residential area just behind Nottingham Castle, and was reluctant to move: fortunately, with the Festival, the two theatres - the Playhouse and the Theatre Royal - and my tours with Sadlers Wells Royal Ballet, there was plenty of freelance work on offer. I stage managed the Royal's 1969 pantomime *Merry King Cole*, with Harry Worth as the bumbling monarch and Peter Butterworth as Dame, and I stage managed and directed for the Playhouse Theatre-in-Education company.

Also at the Playhouse I was company manager for their world premiere production of a new musical developed from Walter Greenwood's novel *Love On The Dole* - previously adapted as a stage play, and a 1943 film starring Deborah Kerr. Director and choreographer for the musical was the formidably-talented (and now Dame) Gillian Lynne, and she almost pulled it off. There was so much good stuff in it: some brilliant dance routines (otherwise why engage Gillian Lynne?); excellent performances from a terrific team of character actors and actresses, clever songs which fitted the plot and a strong story line. Difficult to say, then or now, why it didn't quite work: personally, I wasn't crazy about the stage sets, which relied too much on projections. As an (ex-) lighting man I have never enjoyed working with projections - whether front or back projections. You have to dim down your other lighting, usually that which gives you the shape, the depth, the atmosphere. Some scenes in the recent Royal Ballet production of *Alice in Wonderland* suffered from quite unnecessary projections: ballet is above all a three-dimensional art form. It is essential to accentuate the 'shape' of the choreography, and that can only be done with back- and side-lighting. Remove those so that you can see the projections, and - as happened in *Alice in Wonderland* - the dances and the dancers look 'flat'.

Today, as a speaker, I am equally reluctant to use slides or Powerpoint. Lights in most halls are either on or off: there is never a separate circuit for a spotlight (or two) on the speaker who, as a result, becomes a voice from the darkness. Often there is not even a work-light on the speaker's notes. I am about to present my first-ever illustrated talk *A Trip down the River Charente*, and I'm not looking forward to it. "Welcome to tonight's guest speaker, Brian Freeland. Get a good look at him now because we're about to switch all the lights off".

The Head of Design at Nottingham Playhouse was Patrick Robertson: he had occupied a similar position in Bristol during my National Service days and had designed the production of Becket's play *Waiting for Godot* starring Peter O'Toole which Mick Brown and I had so enjoyed at that time. I suspect that it was Patrick who relayed the message to Stuart Burge that Mr O'Toole might just be interested in doing the play again for - say - a short run in a quality provincial playhouse. However it came about, the production was scheduled, and I was engaged as Company and Stage Manager. The cast would be O'Toole as Vladimir; Donal McCann as Estragon; Niall Toibin as Pozzo and Frank Middlemass as the much-put-upon Lucky. Frank was a member of the resident Playhouse company and had been a bitter-sweet Fool to Michael Hordern's Lear. We rehearsed down in London, and returned to Nottingham to find the three-week run totally Sold Out.

According to the programme the Director was Frederick Monoyer, a hat which O'Toole occasionally wore whenever he wanted to direct himself in a production. I can't guarantee this, but I don't recall that Mr Monoyer ever directed anything that didn't have Peter O'Toole in the cast. Whichever of them directed it, he did an excellent job, and the reviews were overwhelmingly good. Not for the first time at a Sam Becket production Harold Hobson went 'over the top': "*for the length of its run this production makes Nottingham Playhouse the theatrical capital of England*".

Peter's drinking seemed to be under control: he wasn't always ready to answer the 'beginners' call, but nothing serious. Not in the Judy Garland league. And he had agreed to be Guest of Honour at the Playhouse Supporters Club's Annual Dinner and Dance on the evening of the second Sunday. Obviously the Dinner was a sell-out, with the ladies all beautifully turned out, freshly coiffed, ready to meet - perhaps even dance with - Lawrence of Arabia himself.

Well, dinner was finished and cleared away, and there was no sign of Mr O'Toole. The band struck up, the dancing started, but still no Lawrence of Arabia. The evening was almost over by the time our rather-the-worse-for-wear Vladimir wove his way into the hall and onto the platform having spent the evening with the pantomime company from the Theatre Royal in a local hostelry. Dinner finished, dancing over; the only thing left for him to do was to draw the raffle. He desperately tried to focus his eyes on the stationary ticket as his body swayed slowly past it, first one way and then the other. Finally: success. "Blue ticket forty-two". A pause. A long pause. The glazed eyes grew a little tighter; the voice a little tetchier. "Blue ticket forty-two". Another pause. The fixed smile slowly disappeared as the evening drew towards its apparently inevitable conclusion. "Oh fuck 'em" he said, "give us another ticket".

Chapter Twenty-Two: Friends.

 I was Manager of the Adam Smith Theatre in Kirkcaldy in January 1989 when I celebrated my thirtieth year in 'the business'. Peter O'Toole sent me a card: "May you manage another thirty years".

At the start of those first thirty years, in January 1959, Bernard Bresslaw - one of the stars of the London Palladium pantomime, *Sleeping Beauty* - sang *Friends,* a typically cheerful little Cyril Ornadel ditty:

"Friends, isn't it very nice to have friends.
Isn't it very nice to have friends to rely upon,
Shoulders to cry upon,
You must have friends. . ."

I'm sure it must be true in other peripatetic professions, but maintaining close friendships through a career that involves touring the country - or, indeed, the world - as well as (in my case) residencies in Manchester, Pwllheli, Bahrain, Richelieu, Glasgow, Colombo, Beirut, Nottingham, Doha, Stirling, Khartoum or Kirkcaldy can be quite difficult. I'm not thinking so much about those theatricals based in London, where both work and social life can generally be held together via the excellent underground system and bus services.

No, my thoughts are with colleagues who, like myself, spent most of their time away from home. We form a small tight-knit group for a few weeks of rehearsals, followed perhaps by a tour or a short season - all working closely together, living in each other's pockets, dependent on each other for the success of the play or opera or ballet or musical or summer season or pantomime. Then the engagement ends, and everyone goes their separate ways. Some you may never meet again; some only occasionally, whilst others crop up with surprising regularity. Some, it's fair to say, you don't miss, but there are many whose name on a cast list will bring a little buzz of anticipation.

Going back to Scotland is always a pleasure, but an exhausting one. So many good friends, ex-neighbours or former colleagues who all expect a visit, and I'm in trouble if word gets out that I have been anywhere north of the border and haven't called in to see them. The Tod sisters in Coaltown of Wemyss, Alan and Carol in St Andrews, Sandy and Joan in Aberdour, Betty in Stirling, Jane Harrod, my choreographer/stage manager for three busy years, a dozen or so friends in Kirkcaldy and half the population of Dollar - they all keep in touch, particularly at Christmas. What is nice is that when we do meet, however occasionally, the friendship immediately picks up where we left off last time - and with friends overseas that might be after a gap of several years.

When I took up residence in Richelieu, I was tied to the shop and rather dependent on friends visiting me. Some did, notably Murray Melvin who had been one of the stars of Joan Littlewood's company at Stratford East where he is still involved as theatre archivist. He diverted to Richelieu for a couple of days during a holiday in France, and I was able to take him through to visit the nearby town of Loudun. Aldous Huxley's 1952 book *The Devils of Loudun* had been adapted for the stage by John Whiting, and produced by the RSC in

1960 as the second play of their first Aldwych season. Ken Russell 's 1971 film version, drawing on both the book and the play, tells the story of Father Urbain Grandier, libertine; arch-priest of St Pierre du Marché, and leader of the opposition to Cardinal Richelieu. Sister Jeanne, the hunchback abbess of the Ursuline convent, is sexually obsessed with the Priest and accuses him of 'possessing' her. As a result he is charged with bewitching the convent and with having 'dealings with the Devil'. Found guilty, he has his legs crushed, and is then burnt at the stake as Richelieu's troops arrive to destroy the town's defences.

Oliver Reed and Vanessa Redgrave were the stars of the film, and Murray Melvin had the key role of Father Mignon. He was thrilled to be visiting the actual scenes of these real-life events, and even more so when it became obvious that the townsfolk had recognised him. Over lunch we noticed the cafe staff in a huddle, trying to decide if it really was Father Mignon eating in their establishment.

Eventually the manager gave him the 'question direct'; Murray confirmed his identity, and for the rest of the day he got the full star treatment.

The film's combination of religious imagery alongside violent and sexual content caused enormous controversy. Russell cut some explicit nudity, some details of the first exorcism, and part of the crushing of Father Grandier's legs in order to get an X-certificate, but before the studio submitted the print to the British Board of Film Censors they made further cuts, removing two entire scenes. There are countries in the world which have still never seen an unedited version of *The Devils*.

> For me, any mention of *The Devils* instantly recalls the
> old newspaper cartoon showing two genteel, elderly
> ladies looking at a poster for the film, with one of
> them getting very excited and saying
> "Oh we must go and see this, Norah.
> It's by that lovely man who made *The Boy Friend*".

A well-known actress once asked her actor father whether he
had always been true to her mother.
"Of course" he answered, "totally".
"Even on tour?".
"On tour doesn't count".

I'm not denying that it happens; that it has happened. An
actor friend in one of our touring companies, a married man,
fancied a young lady in the management office in whichever
foreign city we happened to be that day. He sent her some
flowers, booked a table for dinner, and eventually had his
wicked way. Next morning he said to me "Now it's your
turn". I said I hadn't realised we were keeping score, "but if
we are then I'm already 2-1 ahead and we're not even
approaching half-time". I offered to get him a list of florists in
the various cities on our tour schedule, but privately
appreciated that in his case, he had made adultery 'count' -
even on tour - and I suspect that I was just a little bit jealous.

So was it all too casual? Apart from the above example,
mostly yes. But when you are on the move all the time, a
different airport and a different city every few days, you take
whatever opportunities are on offer: meals, perhaps; trips to
the beach or a tourist attraction; tickets for a show - and
occasionally something more intimate. It's always
consensual; you both understand the circumstances. There
have been some serious relationships along the way. Bernard
Shaw also had some serious relationships along the way,
quite a lot of them - although looking back towards the end of

his life he admitted that he had only truly been 'in love' twice, once in his youth and once in middle age. He mentioned no names. The first existentialist philosopher, Kierkegaade, said "Life must be lived forwards, but is understood backwards", and that is equally true of love. And sex. You can't really be certain whether you made the right decisions or not until it is too late to do anything about it.

At least, unlike my anonymous actor friend, I didn't have adultery on my conscience: I 'm not married. A moving target is difficult to hit and I was never in the same town or, indeed, the same country long enough to sustain any kind of close stable relationship. Three visits to India in quick succession did set up something which might have developed had we been able to spend more time together. Perhaps I should have sent flowers. When, like Shaw, I looked backwards to understand the relationships which have meant most to me, I realised that all three were entirely chaste.

On my first overseas tour with the Bristol Old Vic the director, Denis Carey, realised that he was short of understudies to cover for accident or delhi-belly. He threw a script at me and said "read that". I sight-read a couple of pages, he took the book back and said "you can't act". It didn't worry me: I had no ambitions to be an actor. Ambitions, yes: to be an actor, no. Similar incidents happened throughout my life: what do you know about theatre management; you're a lighting man? What do you know about script-writing; you're a theatre manager? What do you know about directing; you're a scriptwriter? After directing my third Grand Opera I moved down to East Sussex and, bored, wondered what else I couldn't do.

I discovered that Professor John Pick was a near neighbour. He had started the Arts Administration Diploma Course at City University, and had written many of the standard text books on Arts Administration: I had done the Arts

Administration Degree Course at Central London Polytechnic. With just this tenuous connection I wrote to introduce myself and was invited for coffee. We soon discovered many other connections: we had both performed in the tiny Robin Hood Theatre at Averham, north of Nottingham, for example. Also in Nottingham, we had both worked with stage designers Patrick Robertson and Stephen Doncaster: he at Trent Polytechnic, me at the Playhouse. We share an interest in Music Hall: I am a member of both the British and Scottish Music Hall Societies: he, for many years, was greatly in demand as a Chairman for Old Time Music Hall presentations. Morning coffee became a weekly event, every Monday, as we discovered even more co-incidental connections. He read some of my magazine articles for The Scots Thistle, and said some encouraging things about them (a whole new experience for me: I was expecting "you can't write"). When I told him I was working on a script about the 'Twinkle' producer and pantomime dame Clarkson Rose, he showed me a paragraph about Clarkie's friendship with the notorious Doctor John Bodkin Adams who was alleged to have 'eased the passing' of perhaps one hundred and forty of his elderly female patients. That single paragraph gave me the entire plotline for a new script *See You In Heaven*.

Dr Adams was arrested and tried at the Old Bailey for the murder of just one of his patients, a Mrs Morrell. After a seventeen-day trial he was acquitted, returned to Eastbourne and continued his practice. Many of his old patients went back to him: whenever I mention Bodkin Adams in my talks it is interesting to note how many people comment "Oh, I do hope there's a Dr Adams around when my time comes".

Professor Pick came along to one of these talks, at a Women's Institute meeting. Again, I was expecting "You're not a speaker" - but no. More encouragement. He even passed an engagement on to me when he found that he had been double-booked. Two years ago, only a year after the death from cancer of his wife Ann, John was struck down with Guillain-Barré Syndrome, losing his entire nervous system. He has slowly recovered from that, but after so long in bed the legs have seized up and he has waited with considerably more patience than I would have shown for the operation to un-seize them. However, it has given me the opportunity to return a friend's hospitality and encouragement by helping out with shopping and tea-making, changing bulbs and rewiring plugs. And summoning the fire brigade when the lock inside his front door jammed, and he was trapped inside, alone, in bed. Every afternoon he is hoisted out of that bed - not without some extremely-theatrical yelling and screaming - and into a wheelchair where he, too, is busily engaged with his own memoirs. I look forward to reading them: John was much closer to the seats of power, to the supposed 'decision-makers', whereas I was never much more than a foot-soldier: at best an NCO. Let's hope he names some names.

Mark Pritchard was a colleague, and has been an 'occasional' friend ever since the West End transfer of *Oh What a Lovely War*. Mark worked on the original Stratford East production, and spent several years with the show; he is, I believe, still a member of the board of directors at Stratford. I was at his first wedding. He went on to be a very busy lighting designer, much in demand in Europe and the Scandinavian countries. He recommended me for what turned out to be a very challenging position as stage manager for the Commonwealth Games Arts Festival in Edinburgh, boycotted by some countries because the Thatcher administration was trading with apartheid South Africa. Mark also suffered under Charley Henchis in Beirut, and was involved with the Pitlochry Festival Theatre in Scotland for several summers, not too far from my home in Fife. We don't meet up so often now - he lives with his second wife and family in Nottingham - but he was at the other end of a phone line when I forgot the name of our musical director in Beirut. "Eddie", he said. And then a few minutes later he called me back. "Eddie Guerin".

Mary Evans was a stage manager during my first tour with Scottish Opera; PA to, first, Peter Brook and then the Director of the Northcott Theatre. Later, she and the late Monica Shallis formed the successful Cygnet Training Theatre, based in Exeter where a cup of tea always awaits me whenever I am in that area.

"Friends; isn't it very nice to have friends.... "?

Chapter Twenty-Three: Kirkcaldy to Stratford-on-Avon.

Whilst enjoying the apathetic life of a locus eater lazing by the swimming pool of 'the house with two kittens' I had written two scripts, and the first ten chapters of what, by now, has become the book you are currently reading. When the owners finally took up residence, to the obvious dismay of the cats who had spent two years training me to anticipate their every requirement, it seemed the right time to discover whether my scribblings had any commercial value. My brother Ronald was living in East Sussex, at least the fifteenth generation of our branch of the Freeland family tree to reside in the county, so I headed in that direction and got two summer jobs at Hever Castle - in the Finance Office during the day, and House Manager for the Open Air Theatre in the evenings.

I started to promote my scripts in London, of course - but also in Scotland. My last job in the UK had been in Kirkcaldy, and I knew more people up there than I did in London so at the end of the Hever Castle season I moved up to a small cottage on the estate of the Earl of Wemyss. I also knew a little about the amateur drama scene in central and eastern Scotland, and that was to prove important as I sought groups with the potential to premiere original, large-cast plays.

When I took over the management of Kirkcaldy's Adam Smith Theatre in 1987 I was new to Fife and most of what I knew about the 'Kingdom' I had gleaned from a popular book by author Christopher Rush, *A Twelvemonth and a Day*.
The title is from an anonymous poem:

> *The twelvemonth and a day being up,*
> *The dead begin to speak:*
> *'O who sits weeping on my grave*
> *And will not let me sleep?'*

His book describes the first twelve years in the life of the grandson of a Fife fisherman in parallel with the twelve months of the fishing season, adding the 'day' as a kind of epilogue. It is strongly autobiographical, but weaves in legends and characters from the fishing village of St Monan's where Christopher was born. The Glasgow Herald critic described it as "*powerful, vivid, evocative, funny, awesome, loving and so assured in its writing it catches the breath*".

The characters are so well-drawn, and the dialogues so beautifully-crafted that it was no great surprise when producer Christopher Young and director Ian Sellar decided to make a film of it. *Venus Peter*. A charming, attractive film, shot in the Shetlands with a Stromness schoolboy Gordon R Strachan (no, not that Gordon Strachan) chosen from over a thousand applicants for the role of Peter. Our venue, the Adam Smith Theatre - named for the philosopher and economist who was born in the town - also happened to be the only Regional Film Theatre in Fife, so I sent off an urgent request for a 'preview' screening. The request was granted, with the bonus that author Christopher Rush and producer Christopher Young would attend, and answer questions afterwards. That was my first meeting with Chris Rush, now one of my closest 'occasional' friends, and intrepid collaborator on a series of theatrical adaptations of his works.

The first of these was my stage adaptation of Christopher's book *A Twelvemonth and a Day,* done with his permission and with a great deal of input on his part. The correspondence chasing backwards and forwards between Crail and East Sussex was lengthy and ongoing: when we started to look at songs and other musical inserts Chris sent me a tape of his suggestions that included hymns and sea shanties - some transferred from records, others sung live into his dictaphone with, I was convinced, the gentle tinkle of ice cubes in the background.

Much as I loved the film, I thought that the constant presence of a twelve-year-old boy kept the story in a single time frame, whereas the book quite clearly develops over a twelve year period. My script made use of an older 'narrator', with two youngsters playing the 'boy' (as he is known throughout the book) at ages six and twelve. This allowed for a handful of unusual theatrical moments when the adult 'boy' shared a scene with one of his younger selves.

During my time as Administrator at the MacRobert Arts Centre in Stirling I had directed a 'first division' group, Dollar Drama, in their production of Chekhov's play *Three Sisters*. Their venue didn't have a stage: they had to play on the floor of a school hall, with the audience on temporary raked seating - so temporary that it all had to be packed away every night to clear the hall for assembly and school lunches.

This had encouraged them over the years to be adventurous both in play selection and production style. I offered them the world premiere of our new stage adaptation of *A Twelvemonth and a Day* and, as I had hoped, they jumped at the chance - only realising later that the production would require more performers than they had members. They organised open auditions, and gathered together a superb cast which included some of their own youth drama group.

Cathie Mason, Late President of Dollar Drama:
We learned a great deal from this production. Involving ourselves in our characters and our stage 'family' was helped by our director, and also by the language and construction of the play. It is real and it is poetic. It is funny and moving, and always there is a sense of a close-knit community whose existence is dependent on an industry that is coming to an end. There is a nostalgia for a past way of life, and a sense of continuing values. Times change, and we change with them".

Dollar Drama's production of A *Twelvemonth and a Day*

Christopher didn't attend the rehearsals, and saw the play for the first time at its final performance.
"Authors usually dread the thought of seeing their books filmed or staged. This author was sceptical as well as fearful. In the end I was completely taken by storm by this production. It brought my book to life in a way that I would never have dreamed possible. I saw my whole culture and community pass over the stage, fill mouth and mind and ears with the music of their lives - and then vanish, leaving an empty theatre. It is funny, tragic, moving, spellbinding.

Brian Freeland's stage adaptation has worked a weird magic and the book has undergone a sea-change. This theatre production is a new and astonishing creation".

The annual Scottish Community Drama Association's Festival meant that there was a regular demand for new one-act plays, and I suggested to Chris that we adapt one of his collection of short stories published as *Peace Comes Dropping Slow* (yes, he is a great admirer of Yeats). Being Chris, he offered the one with a supposed witch being chased over the Fife hillsides with her skirts round her waist and boobies exposed to the world. Believing that the SCDA was probably not quite ready for that kind of thing, I looked instead at *Lilies That Fester*, a dark tale involving suspected witchcraft in the Kilrenny Manse. By setting the whole piece in the church vestry, and using short scenes in which the last person on stage at the end of each scene started the next scene, we were able to keep it moving quite swiftly with only the briefest of blackouts to mark the passage of time. Kirkcaldy Amateur Dramatic Society (KADS) took it on, cast it well, and picked up the Benedetti Salver for second place.

The script was entered for the Geoffrey Whitworth Awards, and finished in the top six Best New British One-Act Plays of 2006. Another tale from that same book - *Not Without Honour,* featuring William, the ragged, drunken 'preacher' who stalked the streets and churches of St Monans every Sunday morning - became one of the most memorable scenes in the stage adaptation of *A Twelvemonth and a Day.*

Christopher taught English at George Watson's College in Edinburgh for thirty years where he met and married a colleague, biology teacher Patricia Boyd, and they had two children. He started writing when passed over for the job as Head of Department and needed an outlet for his frustration, and his early works revolved around memories of his birthplace in St Monans "*as I tried to repossess it with words"*. *Peace Comes Dropping Slow* was published in 1983: eight more books and a screenplay followed in the next ten years. Patricia died of cancer in 1993, leaving Christopher alone *"struggling with the washing machine as well as continuing to teach"*, and *"too exhausted to write"*. Only in 2001, when he married Anna, a Russian exchange teacher, and returned to a settled home life was the old creativity rekindled. A new book *To Travel Hopefully* appeared at the end of 2002, around the same time as their first child, Jenny. So imminent was Jenny's arrival that Anna was unable to join Christopher at the last night of *A Twelvemonth and a Day*.

To Travel Hopefully shows Christopher wrestling to cope with Patricia's death. *"Writing it was like opening an old wound: it's a healing thing, almost like a cauterising iron. It heals even as it burns"*. In the remote Cevennes mountain region of southern France he bought a donkey and followed in the footsteps of Robert Louis Stevenson who, also coming to terms with personal heartbreak, had made the same twelve-day odyssey in 1878. Amazingly, this was Christopher's first trip abroad, and his first journey by plane.
"The book was part of a continuing conversation with Patricia, and it was actually Anna who suggested that I should write it. However, I'm not suggesting that everyone enduring bereavement should take a donkey through the Cevennes; apart from anything else the weather was atrocious".

With a replenished zest for living, Chris started work on a fictional biography of William Shakespeare. Since we know so little about him - other than his plays and sonnets - any biography of Shakespeare is bound to be largely fictional. The premise of Christopher's 'novel' *Will* is that a dying William Shakespeare is dictating his own 'will' to his lawyer, Francis Collins. Dictating it in a mad rush in order to prevent Thomas Quiney, the adulterous husband of his daughter Judith, from getting even a sniff of whatever remains following the playwright's demise. Using only the framework of Shakespeare's actual will and the insight gained from teaching Shakespeare for thirty years, Christopher fashioned a 460-page blend of scholarship and imagination which carries a ring of truth: there is a conviction about the descriptions of the school, his father's shop, the abattoir - and especially the central chapters describing William's walk across the City when he first arrives in London - which make you believe that the rest of Christopher's imaginary history could so easily be the truth, the whole truth.

The book was published shortly after *Shakespeare In Love* cleaned up at the Oscars, and immediately attracted the attention of two of our leading screen actor/knights, Ben Kingsley and Kevin Spacey: each, I suspect, seeing a cracking role for themselves as the dying playwright. Kingsley won the first round and bought the full performing rights for five years, but failed to find a suitable script or the finance. He retained the film rights for a further five years, giving Spacey the opportunity to snap up the theatre rights for his then London venue, the Old Vic.

Christopher suggested that we might prepare our own stage adaptation to offer to Kevin Spacey, and at this point we began to understand some of the reasons why Ben Kingsley's film script had not materialised. For a start the novel is a cradle-to-grave story, with Shakespeare aging from birth to a dying 52-year-old. Compare that time span to *Shakespeare In Love* which all happens within a few weeks. Secondly - and this is the major problem for any film or stage adaptation - there is very little conflict in Christopher's biography. *Will* is a wonderfully imagined story, rich in detail, but it moves on from scene to scene without any serious external threats to his life or his work. The death of his son Hamnet is a key moment; the religious disputes and outbreaks of plague interrupt the momentum but appear as minor incidents in such a long, detailed story.

However, we gave it a go. The lifetime aging of the leading character was solved much as we solved it in *A Twelvemonth and a Day* by having the older William as both character and Narrator, with a younger actor playing the more youthful Will. Conflict proved more difficult, but in the draft we offered to Kevin Spacey we had a single actor play several different roles, each role demonstrating a conflicting attitude towards Shakespeare the man, his works or his lifestyle.

We never discovered whether Kevin Spacey liked the adaptation or not, or even whether he had actually read it. *Shakespeare In Love* turned up in the West End in a successful, well-reviewed stage production, and that was probably the final nail in the coffin of our stage adaptation of *Will*. However, we still have a few copies of that early draft: Sir Kevin's rights have now expired, and if anyone is sufficiently interested ....?

In fact, as I write, we are taking a fresh look at the whole project. Christopher's latest book *Penelope's Web* has just hit the bookstalls and *Around The World In Eighty Plays* is on the way to the publishers, offering us both a brief opportunity to attempt a different style of staging for his fictional biography. The multi-scene, enormous cast, cradle-to-grave epic is slowly morphing into a small-cast (seven), single-set, real-time drama. Shakespeare's lawyer Francis Collins has given way to a stronger 'co-star' in the form of fellow-playwright Ben Jonson. "If you can't accept the concept of ghosts, don't direct Hamlet" someone once wrote. Well, we don't exactly have a ghost - but we have introduced a new character who may, or may not, be of this world.

Will it work? *Nous verrons.* We'll see.

Chapter Twenty-Four: From Taillebourg to Lewes.

It is so easy to fall into the trap of writing about 'the English' and 'the French' as though both were always unitary countries, which, of course, they weren't. And easy to assume that the English all lived in England, and the French all lived in France - which, of course, they didn't. If like me you failed History 'O' level, and only know King Henry II and his family from the play *The Lion in Winter*, then you might assume that he was very English (or even Irish if you only saw Peter O'Toole in the film version) and that he had four sons. In fact he was born in Le Mans, died in Chinon, and he had eight legal children (five sons and three daughters) as well as two admitted illegitimate sons - Geoffrey, Archbishop of York and William, Earl of Salisbury. The last two gave strong support to the King during the 'Great Revolt' when his legitimate sons - Richard, Geoffrey and John, together or separately - fought for more land, more power, more money. The Queen, Eleanor of Aquitaine, often had a hand in her sons' conspiracies.

I suppose it started to get confusing when William the Conqueror invaded in 1066. William was not king of France, but merely Duke of Normandy. The King of France at that time was a fourteen-year-old Philip 1st: technically, the Duke of Normandy was his vassal, and if the Duke of Normandy became King of England then - technically - the King of England was also his vassal. This dispute would bedevil relationships between the relevant holders of these various titles for generations.

William the Conqueror was crowned in Westminster Abbey on Christmas Day, and the coronation service was conducted in French - or, presumably, Norman, since there wasn't a recognised French language until King Francois sorted that out five hundred years later. Norman nobles settled in England (probably on confiscated estates), and English nobles found their way across the channel. Inter-marriages brought dowries, and sometimes titles. William never integrated his two domains, and was succeeded by a pair of his sons: the eldest, Robert Curthose, as Duke of Normandy, and the second (surviving) son, William Rufus, as King of England, William II. He was killed in the New Forest in 1100 and succeeded by another brother Henry I. Henry I deposed his elder brother Robert and reunited the titles of England's King and Normandy's Duke. When Henry I died in 1135 the Conqueror's grandson Stephen of Blois, a wealthy Norman with estates in Kent, inherited both titles - and that's when the troubles first started.

Henry's daughter, Matilda, felt she had a claim to the English throne, and in this she was supported by her family - husband Geoffrey of Anjou; half-brother Robert, Duke of Gloucester, and son Henry (born in Le Mans - yes, that Henry, Peter O'Toole's Henry). Still only twenty years of age, Henry invaded England in 1153, and a weakened King Stephen made a peace treaty naming Henry as his successor.

A year later, Stephen was dead and Henry II added King of England and Duke of Normandy to his other titles - Count of Anjou, Count of Maine and Count of Naples. Then he married Eleanor and acquired yet another title, Duke of Aquitaine. Later he added the Lordship of Ireland, and these territories together became known as the Angevin Empire.

History on the whole seems to have been kinder to Henry the King than to Henry the father. He is credited with laying the foundations of an English legal system, and the beginnings of an English nation, possibly even a British nation through his dealings with the Welsh, Scots and Irish. Controlling a vast empire in the days of horses and sailing ships meant, however, that he needed reliable lieutenants, instead of which he had quarrelsome sons and a devious wife.

His first son, William, died at two years old; his second, Henry, was crowned as 'the Young King', presumably to look after things while his father was abroad but the histories suggest he was happier as a star of the jousting tournaments: *"the best king of England who ever took up a shield"*. The Young King died in 1183 of dysentery, aged twenty-eight; Prince Richard became heir apparent, but not 'young king' - yet another grievance. Prince John was sent to sort out Ireland, and made a mess of it; he lost his lands in Normandy and, after succeeding his brother Richard I as King, upset the Barons and was forced to sign the Magna Carta. *"Sinfully lustful and lacking in piety"*, he had a string of illegitimate children during his first marriage, but a happier second marriage (and five children) with the (very) much younger Isabella of Angouleme. Their eldest son, nine years old at the time of John's death became King Henry III, with William Marshall as Protector.

Anyone driving direct from Saintes to Rochefort would miss the attractive, picturesque Charente village of Taillebourg, where these historic details are particularly relevant. Go by boat: it's more leisurely and you can tie up at the quayside; once busy with commercial shipping, now mostly occupied by fishermen. Taillebourg was the scene of the 1242 battle between England's King Henry III and Louis IX of France. The bridge at Taillebourg is a key crossing point over the Charente, guarded by the huge Chateau high on the cliffs above the river. King Louis installed his troops in the Chateau. Henry III was heading towards Saintes when the two armies met at the bridge. The French won this latest skirmish in the great history of the Hundred Years War.

This bridge was the only crossing place for pilgrims heading south on the Camino de Compostela, the pilgrim's route from Saint-Jean-d'Angely towards Santiago de Compostela, the alleged burial place of the apostle James in north-west Spain. Since the valley was often in flood at this point, a long Causeway was built to keep their feet dry. The causeway is still in reasonable condition, if a little overgrown with weeds.

The fortifications surrounding the Chateau de Taillebourg had been demolished during an earlier pre-1242 battle for control of the bridge, leaving only the tower to dominate the heights above the village. Trying to find a position to photograph this tower I found that the frame included a house undergoing renovation: when I congratulated the builder on his excellent workmanship he reminded me that his creamy-coloured stones had been transported from further up-river by lorry, much as they had been transported by *gabarre* for the other buildings in that street hundreds of years previously. The name of the street? *Rue Alienor d'Aquitaine.*

Cruise on to the next village, Port d'Envaux, and you'll probably find the old commercial quay busy with pleasure cruisers and houseboats but you can tie up along the left bank below the gardens of a row of impressive houses built by, and for, the owners of the ships which once traded on the river. Climb up the slope to the main street, and you will immediately realise from the size and quality of these houses that commercial shipping on the Charente must have been an extremely profitable enterprise. To the west of the village, on the road to Plassy, you can find an extraordinary new cultural experience. Within a former limestone quarry, artists from all over the world spend their summers carving huge stone sculptures on the white cliff walls, creating an ever-growing art space. The inspiration behind *Les Lapidiales* is actor/designer/sculptor Alain Tenenbaum: the site opened only in 2001:one of the first sculptures was the keel of a boat, a reminder of the importance of the Charente to the village.

Dine at one of Port d'Envaux's *auberges*, or continue downstream and enjoy, as I did, an excellent lunch at the Hotel Saint-Savinien in the village of the same name, a village with another unusual tourist attraction. The Charente divides and turns back on itself at this point, forming an island, *l'ile de la Grenouillette*, or Little Frog Island. In the middle of that island is a lake which, since 1986, has been home to a Miniature Port. Beautiful hand-crafted boats allow the children to cruise around this delightful setting - with the boats, bridges and other scenic details all designed and built by Jean-Louis Foucaud, a former shipwright. Jean-Louis claims to be retired, but at the time of writing is still building his final boat. This will be named in honour of his daughter Stephanie, who has taken over the management of Saint-Savinien's Miniature Port. The ships are scale models of tug boats, cargo ships and Mississippi paddle-steamers, and the whole experience just feels so professional compared to the Peter Pan's Pool of my own boyhood boating days in Catford.

Port d'Envaux - Saint Savinien

Losing the Battle of Taillebourg in 1242 didn't make Henry III a better warrior: he also lost the Battle of Lewes, back in Britain, in 1264. Carrying on where his father King John left off, he also upset the Barons. Led by Simon de Montfort, 6th Earl of Leicester, the Barons surrounded Lewes Castle on all four sides. Henry's son Edward (later Edward 1) led a cavalry charge against one of the four armies, but chased them so far that he left his father without cover and Henry was overwhelmed by the other three. By the time Edward's cavalry returned they were too exhausted to be of much help.

On his way to Lewes, Henry had stopped off at Robertsbridge Abbey, home to a strict order of Cistercian monks (originally from Burgundy), and known as the White Monks as their cassocks were made from unbleached wool. The King exhorted large sums of money from the unfortunate monks, and the timing of this visit may have been connected with the 1264 Charter of Robertsbridge Abbey which included amongst its signatories a William Frelend - one of the earliest references I have found to our family name. Or the earliest reference to our family name in that 'English' form. There was an earlier reference in 1204, in Chichester, to a Hugh le Frilende. Hugh was a French name (a Norman name?); a corruption of the Germanic Hugo. On the instructions of William the Conqueror, Chichester Cathedral took over from Selsey Abbey in 1075 as the Seat of the South Saxon (Sussex) See of the Church, so there is a strong possibility that Hugh le Frilende was a Norman, either a new arrival or a descendent of a 1066 invader. The villages close to Robertsbridge Abbey are all developed around Norman churches, suggesting that the villages were built to house the Conqueror's followers - who probably included both administrators and soldiers.

The earliest available official Parish records (1538) show numerous Freeland families living in the Norman villages of Brightling and Salehurst. Most are shown as farm labourers, as, probably, were the great majority of William's conquering army. This is pure surmise on my part, but other early references to de Frylonde, and de Frelende in Sussex all help to support my belief that we might be descended from the Normans. Bernard Shaw thought that he might be descended from the Macduffs: I suspect that, so long after the event, neither of our claims will ever be proven. Another common surname in that area is 'French', which may or may not be an argument in my favour. Being even-handed, I have to admit that the list of names of those accompanying the Conqueror at the time of the invasion does not include anything remotely resembling Freeland or even de Frylonde - but then it would have listed only the nobles, and we were never that.

It's not quite in the same league as a Norman invasion or war with the Barons, but I did get caught up in a civil conflict during one of my overseas contracts. I had been invited back to Addis Ababa in 1974 to advise the Ethiopian National Theatre staff on some possible improvements to their technical facilities, and landed at the airport at the same time as plane-loads of Cuban soldiers. They had arrived to assist in the Derg's take-over of the country following the overthrow of Emperor Haile Sellassie. I had a phone call one morning from the British Council advising me not to leave my city centre hotel as there was trouble in the streets. Something I already knew: I could see the roadblocks from my window, and even heard the occasional gunshot. The following morning all was quiet. The Director of the National Theatre collected me in his car and, as we drove to work, I asked what it felt like to be living and working under these conditions. He quietly lifted up a map lying by the gear lever, and showed me a loaded pistol hidden beneath it. "If they stop me, I'll try to take one of them with me" he said. If that was meant to re-assure me, then it really didn't work.

What I genuinely learned from that visit to Addis Ababa, and from a much later working trip to Damascus, was that the ordinary people are generally more concerned about the daily problems of family life - putting food on the table; clothing the children, getting to work or school - than the shenanigans of their politicians and revolutionaries.

Chapter Twenty-Five: Oh Noh it isn't.

What I learned from my visit to Japan was that in Tokyo, even after midnight and without a car in sight, you do not cross the road until the pedestrian lights turn green. I made that mistake one night: returning to the hotel after a late performance I crossed the road against a red light and received an outburst from an upstairs window that needed no translation. I was in Japan as stage manager with the London Shakespeare Group: it was 1977 and we were touring the main cities with a production of *Romeo and Juliet* under the auspices of the British Council, and with sponsorship from the Tokyo Shimbun (newspaper).

One of the first things you discover in Japan is that they really do have problems with their Ls and their Rs - it's something to do with not having an exact equivalent to either of those sounds in their own language. Anyway, it didn't take long before we were referring to Shakespeare's star-crossed lovers as Lomeo and Juriet. We did one performance in a girl's school: the actors finished as usual with two quick bows and then turned and headed towards the dressing room. The Headmistress ran after them: "you must come back; you must come back. The girls, they are still crapping".

The tour gave us nine days in Tokyo. In an effort to squeeze in as much Japanese theatre as possible I went to matinees, late night shows and two shows on Sunday, our free day. In this way I managed to fit eight productions around our own evening performances. Two were traditional - Noh Theatre and Kabuki: impenetrable but impressive. One was quite bizarre - a full song and dance spectacular with a large, all-female cast, half of them in 'drag'. Fast-moving, professional, beautifully-dressed and - for whatever reason - Sold Out.

Two good friends, Robin Lawrence and Nigel Lawton, were regular, and always welcome, visitors to my Scottish theatres with their Presto Puppet productions, and I was keen to see some Japanese puppet theatre. One of these was in a style quite new to me with the operators sitting on small mobile stools. One hand supports the puppet's body; the other hand is actually down one of the puppet's sleeves, in view, and used to handle props or weapons. The puppet's feet are connected to the operator's slippers. As the puppet 'walks' the stool is wheeled around the stage. This clever, imaginative presentation included a most realistic sword fight.

However, the show which made by far the greatest impression on me was a contemporary production in a packed sweltering basement theatre, developed around the theme of the manipulation of talent by Svengali-like 'directors and managers'. I confess that I didn't recognise all of the references, but Marilyn Monroe, Judy Garland and Nijinsky were certainly in there. Some wonderful imagery from both the performers and the design team.

Our production of *Romeo and Juliet* had toured the Indian sub-continent the previous year, but there had been a couple of cast changes - one being Romeo himself. It wasn't until our first performance in Japan that they realised that our replacement Romeo needed new tights - a problem compounded by the fact that he had forgotten to pack a jock-strap. A friend, ballet teacher and choreographer Frank Freeman, was in Tokyo wearing his other hat as Examiner for the Royal Academy of Dance: he introduced me to a married couple, local ballet dancers and teachers. Tokyo buildings are so densely packed together that shopping malls go upwards rather than sideways, and they told me to look for the Mall with the 'Americaya Shoe Shop' on the ground floor. "Americaya is our way of saying American", they explained. Two floors above that I would find what I needed. "The Americaya Jock-strap Shop?" I suggested. Not quite that, but a dance-wear shop that would certainly have what I was looking for. It did, and Romeo gave a much more confident performance that evening, smartly-dressed and well-supported in every way.

Even in a ballet world which is chock-full of charming, hardworking people, Frank Freeman was exceptional. A talented dancer with both the Royal Ballet and English National Ballet; patron and choreographer for the National Youth Ballet, but above all a wonderful, enthusiastic dancing teacher and examiner. Much-loved and, since his untimely death in 2011, much-missed. RIP, Frank.

Japan is a country of contrasts: the colour and beauty of Kyoto's temples and gardens compared with the grey desolation of Hiroshima; the speed of the Bullet Train between cities compared with the sluggish movement of traffic in Tokyo. There was an overhead motorway through the centre of the city with, invariably, stationary vehicles. A resident described it as the longest, thinnest car park in Japan.

We performed in a contrasting variety of venues including a badminton court in a school gymnasium with limited technical facilities, and a proper theatre with full technical facilities but none of them working. The lighting control system? "Not work". The sound system? "Not work". The theatre technician? "Not work". These were most surprising in a country renowned for its technical expertise but, to be fair, they were the exceptions. Generally, everything ran smoothly and efficiently, and everyone was most friendly and helpful - especially my technical assistant. He was usually late for the morning bus departure and would come racing down the street, skid to a halt and make a quick formal bow before apologising for his tardiness and then jumping onto the bus.

I particularly welcomed the colourful display of plastic meals outside every restaurant. I tried to learn colours and numbers in every country so that I could get the right 'gels' in the spotlights, and the right circuit numbers on the lighting control board, but colours and numbers are not much help when you want to order dinner in a Japanese restaurant. That is made so much easier when you can just point to a plastic model of your preferred dish.

Sometimes you go into a show not knowing what to expect, and come out delighted, enchanted and entranced by the experience. This happened to me in 1986 in Edinburgh at a performance by the Himawari Children's Theatre Company. They used no make-up or props, no sound tapes, no musical instruments - and only a few words (English and Japanese) - but they performed three Grimm's Tales using just simple costumes and tremendous imagination as they became horses, bears, princes, furniture, wizards and even a lake-full of swans. The Himawari Theatre Group was formed in Tokyo in 1952, and produced many plays for children based on both western and Japanese stories. Their Grimm's trilogy, *The Bewitched Princes*, had been adapted and directed by Yukio Sekiya.

When the British Council informed me that the company would be returning to Britain in 1989 I immediately booked them for the Adam Smith Theatre in Kirkcaldy, where I was then manager - and had no trouble arranging sponsorship with Nissan. A happy, talented and hard-working group, they were rewarded with a Civic Reception and tour of the Town House arranged for them by Provost Robert King.

In the late 1980s the Edinburgh Festival hosted three stunning productions by the Toho Company from Japan. Their director, Yukio Ninagawa, usually gets most of the plaudits, but it was clear that producer Tadao Nakane, designer Kappa Seno and lighting designer Sumio Yoshii all deserved their share of the credit for a series of beautifully-conceived and brilliantly-staged performances. The 1985 Festival saw them in the confines of the Royal Lyceum Theatre with Shakespeare's *Macbeth*. Thirty years ago and only patchily-remembered so the quotes are not mine, but by Irving Wardle, written closer to the event. In my memory the setting was a dark flight of steps, the background to a series of brilliant images: a great branch of orange blossom, for instance, cross-lit against the blackness (some still call it 'the orange blossom Macbeth). One scene had actors riding skeletal horses through pink floating candles making a 'pathway' down the steps.

Irving Wardle:

"The production was piercingly beautiful, and became a legend overnight. Text and scenic language were Japanese, but the emotions were directly accessible. Western drama delivers a present-tense narrative; Noh drama recalls events that are long past. The sleep-walking Lady Macbeth was at once a present-tense dramatic character and a Noh-theatre ghost. In Ninagawa's productions the two traditions come together so that you see the story in double focus. The past runs in tandem with the present; actuality with dream".

In 1986 their venue was the University of Edinburgh; the production *Medea*. Greek tragedy outdoors, where it began, allowing a large red-draped chorus to swoop, unconfined, within the classical backdrop of the Adam, Courtyard.

"Who will forget the death exit of Mikijiro Hira racing up the granite steps, a sword glittering above his head, and vanishing through the black doorway as the chorus flew after him with cries of lamentation? Or his final appearance, enthroned in the dragon chariot high over the balustraded roof, making his departure into the night sky?"

Back indoors in 1988, to the Playhouse - where even Edinburgh's largest stage proved too small for Ninagawa's *Tempest*. The enchanted island overflowed into the wings and into the auditorium: in my front row seat my knees were tucked under the forestage. Ariel flew from tree to tree; boats arrived to disgorge passengers, and I really felt part of the action. So much going on in that enormous space; you often didn't know which way to look.

"Prospero inhabits a waking dream. As director of a desert-island Noh stage he recruits the other characters into his private theatricals assisted by a stage-managerial Ariel. When disengaged, he takes a seat by the musicians, following the events in a prompt copy as though his own future were already down on paper. Then comes his little magic show for the lovers, and the key to Ninagawa's own production.

Beginning with a sequence of common chords in steadily mounting crescendo, the masque turns into a choral ballet developing into an intense, yearning image of perfect human harmony. At its height Prospero recalls the plot against his life - the only event outside his theatrical control - and cancels the ideal vision to deal with earthly reality".

The *ideal vision* of these three incredibly imaginative productions dazzled me, and then frustrated me as, in their wake, came a return to the *earthly reality* - the on-going struggle to stage shows in inadequate venues with tiny budgets and overstretched technicians. Even when I hit the 'big-time' with a resident post at the National Theatre it had been part of a cost-cutting exercise. If you sense the presence of the green-eyed monster then it's with reason. So often I have felt like Nemorino in *L'Elisir d'Amore* when he dreams of marrying Adina - if only he had the money....

But life is not an opera. Or even a Noh play. Oh Noh it isn't!

Chapter Twenty-Six: From Rochefort to Athens

I had started this meandering trip at the river's source, and my finishing line was always intended to be the huge sweeping arches of Rocheforts's viaduct bridge, the final crossing over the River Charente. I arrived in Rochefort on a fairly dull day with a chill wind, and rain always threatening - but determined to do the final stretch on foot.

The Tourist Office gave me a route past the Naval Museum and along the Charente Way (*Chemin de Charente*), which followed the wide - and tidal - river as it flowed towards Rochefort's two bridges. On the other side of the footpath was an apparently-static stream, green with floating weeds which seemingly hid hundreds of clearly-frustrated frogs, all emitting loud and urgent mating calls.

The river takes a long, slow bend, but eventually you get your first glimpse of the Transporter Bridge, built in 1900 as their first attempt to get traffic across the waterway without delaying the deep-water shipping making its way in and out of Rochefort Harbour. Two huge metal towers with a kind of railway right at the top transporting a swaying cradle across at a lower level. A cradle designed to carry motor transport as well as carts, people and animals.

By the 1960s *Le Pont Transbordeur* was carrying 1200 vehicles a day but had reached its limit, and the decision was taken to build a new road bridge. The section of road crossing the river, a span of 92 metres, could be hoisted high in the air to allow ships to pass underneath. That opened in 1967, but long delays for the road traffic while the bridge section was being raised and lowered led to the design for the present curved viaduct which finally opened in 1991. Within a few months the old bridge and approach roads had all been removed. The viaduct is slowly revealed as you walk around the bend; a gently curving structure with a huge arch as the central section carrying traffic high above the shipping lane.

The Transporter Bridge, the last of its kind in France, was declared a national Monument in 1976, restored in 1994, and now carries foot passengers and bicycles - although it was *en panne* (broken down) on the day of my visit. Still following the footpath I passed through one of the smaller arches of the viaduct at 7.00pm on a dull May evening. Journey's end. I was ready for a shower, a meal and a celebratory glass of wine, but they had to wait until I walked all the way into the town, to the hotel, hoping the rain would hold off until I got there. Next morning there were odd flashes of sunshine between the clouds as I took a quick look around Rochefort. There was no river crossing at this point until 1900, so the entire city is on the right bank, to the west of the river, and was essentially a commercial port with a safe, sheltered harbour handling both river and export traffic.

A rare photo showing all three bridges shortly after the opening of the Viaduct, and just before the removal of the central 'lifting span' bridge.

In 1666 Jean-Baptiste Colbert, Finance Minister to the Sun King Louis XIV, proposed Rochefort as the site for a shipyard. But not just any old shipyard. Colbert was consolidating Richelieu's intentions to re-affirm the absolute power of the monarchy, particularly by developing Rochefort as the base for *une marine de guerre*: his shipyard was to be capable of constructing up to 550 vessels for the King's new navy. *Le plus bel arsenal*: the most exceptional naval dockyard on the Atlantic coast. The first of the warships to be completed was named *La Charente*.

Colbert planned all the infrastructures, including an impressive Corderie Royal making all the ropes for the new navy, as well as a new city centre planned on the grid pattern rather like New York or Edinburgh's new town. By 1722 they had added the world's first naval college, but the city had a darker side - in 1766 Rochefort became home to the country's third penal settlement. Designed for 500 chained prisoners, it eventually held nearly five times that number.

The first French submarine was launched there in 1863 and the last, Rochefort's final warship, in 1919: the dockyards closed in 1927.

During WW2 the city was occupied by the Nazis from 1940: and the harbour dynamited and burnt in 1944. The Corderie Royale was threatened with demolition until Culture Minister Andre Malraux classified it as *a historic building in peril* and it reopened as a Museum in 1985. Much of this history is revisited and explained in the excellent *Musée de la Marine* close to the harbour - although the museum staff on duty at the time of my visit had not heard of Jean-Baptiste Colbert.

The shipyard became alive again, attracting over four million visitors, during the construction of a replica frigate, *Hermione*, a copy of the warship built there in 1799 and which carried Marquis Lafayette to America to assist George Washington in his fight for Independence. *Hermione*'s twenty-six cannon were cast by the same Ruelle foundry which had supplied the originals but not, as then, floated down the Charente on board *gabarres*. Sadly *Hermione* sailed just three weeks before my arrival: it was scheduled to visit several cities up the eastern seaboard of the United States before returning to Rochefort at the end of August 2015. However, there was an alternative replica ship in the harbour - a copy of The Nao Victoria, the *caravelle* which carried Magellan on the very first trip around the world.

I've already mentioned the start of my own first trip around the world; travelling across Australia with actor Max Adrian. That tour continued through the Far East, and on across Sri Lanka and India. We finished up in Israel - a very confusing experience which will not be repeated. Our Israel shows were staged both in conventional theatres and in historic sites such as an ancient vaulted cellar in Akko. Laurier Lister, who had directed *An Evening with GBS* back in the UK, came out to Israel for these final performances. Laurier and Max had a holiday planned, so once I had arranged return transport for the costumes my duties were done and I also took a short break - my first experience of Club-Med. An extremely enjoyable experience. Good food, good facilities, and an open-air recorded classical music concert for an hour every evening, ending around sunset. Perfect. And all paid for with coloured beads.

I had, through a Tel Aviv agency, arranged some work with a film company. They were making a TV film about the first Israeli Prime Minister David Ben Gurion, and I was engaged both as production assistant, and to play the small role of a British Army Officer (riding a horse, as I discovered later). There was a minor cast revolt because some of the extras didn't look sufficiently Jewish (the director wasn't Jewish), and then our supposedly-experienced lighting cameraman sent back a day's filming which was seriously overexposed. The money ran out, they had to stop shooting, and I returned to Nottingham, to another short-term contract, but a few weeks later I had to ask for some days off: the Israeli company had found more cash and, since I had already appeared in some scenes, they needed me back for another two days filming. There was a car to meet me at the airport, a hotel room booked: I felt quite important - for two days.

In 1967, with another 'occasional' friend and former colleague, David Sculpher, I got caught up in a film being shot on a Greek beach near Athens. *The Day the Fish Came Out* was written, produced and directed by Michael Cacoyanis, who also designed the costumes, such as they were. A real-life incident in Spain when the Americans lost a couple of atomic bombs in the sea had been transposed to Greece, with Tom Courtenay and Colin Blakely, as the two hapless, unfortunate airmen. Doubly unfortunate, since they spent much of the film clad only in wet Y-fronts. Sam Wanamaker, Candice Bergen and Ian Ogilvy were the other stars. The composer was Mikis Theodorakis who, like the film cameraman Walter Lassally, had previously worked with Cacoyanis on *Zorba The Greek*, a big popular success. *The Day the Fish Came Out* wasn't a popular success. The film is listed as a Greek-British comedy: but I don't remember many laughs in the scenes we were involved in. Halliwell's Film Guide described it as "*addle-pated, would-be satirical mod fantasy*" and I'll take their word for it. David and I were 'extras', cast as hedonistic tourists. Fairly unlikely casting for both of us, being somewhat older and considerably less sleek than the bikini- and briefs-clad youngsters sharing the beach. I remember one all-night filming session in a huge open air cafe when we had so many retakes that maestro Cacoyanis suddenly realised they were running out of food, at which point we received our one and only directorial instruction from him. "Don't eat the props".

Chapter Twenty-Seven: Heading for Home.

Having travelled the length of the Charente, passed under the viaduct at Rochefort, completed my research, and taken my photos it was time to head for home - but with a few brief stops to make along the way. First of those stops was La Rochelle, to check out the city's connections with Cardinal Richelieu. In the early 17th century La Rochelle was the capital of Protestantism in France, controlling its own military alliances and trading privileges. Louis XIII wished to re-unite his kingdom under Catholic control, and entrusted Cardinal Richelieu to lay siege to La Rochelle.

On the landward side, French engineers isolated the city with 12 kilometres of trenches, 11 forts and 18 redoubts, manned by 30,000 troops. Out at sea, 4,000 workmen built a sea-wall 1400 metres long on foundations of sunken hulks filled with rubble, the idea of Royal architect Clement Metezeau. This was manned by the French artillery. In 1628 two English fleets under Earls Denbigh (April) and Lindsay (August) attempted to lift the siege, but failed. By October, with 22,000 out of a population of 27,000 lost to disease, famine and casualties, the city capitulated in unconditional surrender - a victory furthering Richelieu's plans of absolute monarchy for King Louis XIII.

With the end of the siege the battlements were pulled down, but the towers each side of the harbour entrance remain, and dominate the area. By the end of the century La Rochelle harbour was perhaps the busiest in France, mainly because of its involvement in the 'triangular' (slave) trade: goods to Guinea, slaves to the West Indies, sugar to France. Nowadays it is a busy bustling city, extremely welcoming, with plenty to see and do: excellent restaurants, great market, remarkable cathedral with some fascinating exhibits for those with a particular interest in the city's history. The staff at the tourist office could not have been more helpful.

I should like to have stayed longer but I was booked into a little *chambre d'hôte* in Arcais, in the Marais Poitevin, for two nights of rest and rehearsal prior to talks in Beaufort-en-Vallée and Orléans. Mine host was monsieur Jean Leyssene, aged 83, retired farmer, and a great character. The Marais Poitevin is one of Europe's largest marshland areas, covering over 110,000 hectares, and is often referred to as France's *Venise Vert* (Green Venice). Once covered by the sea, the marshes were first drained in the Middle Ages via a complex series of canals - with the islands between the canals used as 'fields' for growing crops and grazing the cows.

But not for milking the cows. They had to be brought back each afternoon to farm buildings which were in the centre of the village. Jean's barns are - were - opposite his house, in the same narrow street as several other houses. Jean will show you photos of himself rowing the cows along the canals in a flat-bottomed 'barge' to whichever grassy island he was using that day, having milked them and then walked them through the village streets to the 'port' for loading. In the afternoon, he would row them home and march them back through the streets for milking, before bedding them down for the night. Eventually, public and civic pressure put an end to the twice-daily movement of livestock through the streets, and to the presence of cowsheds in residential areas. Some of Jean's barns are now garages and sheds; some are homes for his extended family. There are children everywhere, and grandfather Jean does the school run twice a day. Three rooms in the farmhouse were turned into *chambres d'hôte*: since the death of his wife two years ago Jean has done all the cleaning and laundry. Breakfast is at 8.30am, because that is when he collects the bread, and there is a communal kitchen for use by the guests should they not fancy any of the village restaurants. One of the guide books describes the rooms as *chambres modestes, sobrement decorées*. Well, maybe they are. But they are cheap, and clean - and heavily booked because most of his guests return time and time again. Jean is such an interesting guy, and the perfect host. Book early to avoid disappointment.

You'll enjoy the village, too. Arcais has a pretty church and a helpful tourist office (with Wi-Fi, which Jean doesn't have). The 'port' is now busy with boats for hire, with or without a 'rower', and there are two wonderful wooden cranes which confirm that the canal barges used to carry more than cows. Make your leisurely way around the canals, and picnic where Jean's cows used to graze.

Beaufort-en-Vallée is on the road between Angers and Saumur: I went via Saumur because it was Saturday, Market Day, and I wanted to see if anything had changed in the twenty years since I last sold marmalade and chocolate biscuits in the market. There was scaffolding all over the

Church of St Pierre which dominates one end of the market square, and the English lady who sold fresh watercress had moved on - but otherwise it all looked pretty familiar. Part of the market is indoors: several empty shops in that section, although the butcher was still there, and still busy.

Parts of the street market and a public building in Saumur

Lunch in a cafe with Wi-Fi so that I could check my e-mails, and then it was time to go to work - a talk to the Loire Valley English-Speaking Union. They had chosen my talk *Women of the Raj*, about the British women in India prior to Independence, and had booked an Indian caterer to add some spice to the proceedings. The meeting and eating would be in the spacious garden of two of their members Alain and Chantal Bertrand: no ordinary garden since - as well as a magnificent swimming pool - it contained a restored sixteenth century chapel, the venue for the talk. There was also an extremely well-finished and well-furnished *gîte*, or granny wing, where I would be spending the night - after our charming and well-organised hostess, Chantal, had supervised the washing of the crockery, cutlery and glassware, and the return of all the furniture.

A memorable evening, and a memorable breakfast the next morning with Alain. Formerly with SNCF, he was Chief Operating Officer when the Channel Tunnel opened in 1994, and held a series of senior posts with Eurotunnel over the next eleven years - Deputy Managing Director; Director of

Railway Services, and finally Director of the Infrastructure Division with responsibility for maintenance, real-time operations and safety. In 1999 he was involved with the commercial arrangement which led to the fibre-optic connection between England and France being routed through the tunnel: in 2002 he led Eurotunnel's court application to have the Sangatte refugee camp closed down, and is still, ten years after retirement, concerned about the ongoing asylum-seeker problem. I asked if he had any views about HS2, and he was very positive: "it will re-route all the express traffic, and permit a much better service on the existing lines".

I've had a strangely episodic life and career, largely unplanned, and therefore full of surprises. Nothing more surprising, though, than being hosted on successive nights by two such interesting men, fascinating characters, and as diversely experienced as Messieurs Jean Leyssene and Alain Bertrand.

Chapter Twenty-Eight: The End is Nigh.

I was in France when my father died, in 1972. The Nottingham Playhouse Company was scheduled to tour France that year, and I suggested to the city's Junior Chamber of Commerce (of which I was a relatively-new member) that we should hire a Corporation double-decker bus, fit it out as a mobile publicity exhibition for the City, and follow the route of the theatre company. Which, amazingly, happened. My colleague David Sculpher and I had driving lessons with the Corporation's instructor. The French *Chambres* assisted with local arrangements, usually by finding a town centre site for the bus, and organising local publicity, although the Paris *Chambre* also laid on an official lunch for our visiting guests - the Lord Lieutenant of Nottinghamshire and our Branch President, John Crosse. The project was mainly funded through the sale of display spaces on the bus to firms and organisations from both the City and County.

On the way to the ferry we stopped off at my parent's home in Balham and gave them a quick tour of the exhibition, then pushed on to Dover where the ferry captain refused to load the bus because the seas were a bit rough and he was afraid that with its soft springing the bus might not stay upright. I explained our tight schedule, with a site and a press reception awaiting us within a few hours; even then he would allow us on only if I signed a disclaimer on behalf of the Nottingham Junior Chamber of Commerce accepting full responsibility for any damage to the bus during the crossing. You, the readers, are the first to know this: that information has never been revealed either to the Junior Chamber or to Nottingham Corporation. David reversed the bus all the way down the ramp, and the ferry staff then slung a long rope around it and tied it to one side of the car deck.

Paris was the third stop on the tour: we had arranged overnight parking in the Embassy courtyard, but couldn't get the bus past an ornamental hanging light in the driveway so had to park it in the street. I went to their hotel to await the arrival of the Lord Lieutenant and our Branch President: they were later than expected since the advertised 'direct flight from Nottingham to Paris' actually landed at Beauvais and they had to complete the journey by bus. They arrived with the devastating news that my father was dead, the result of a heart attack.

As I explained near the start of this book, dad had an operation for tuberculosis, followed by a long period in a sanatorium. Until his illness, he had been a heavy smoker. Having suffered a collapsed lung, he was never really fully fit again and, unable to exercise, he was overweight. He was also a natural worrier - I would joke sometimes that he would worry about having nothing to worry about - and his last sight of me was at the wheel of a double-decker bus setting off down Bellamy Street on the way to France where they drive on the wrong side of the road. He had seen me off to Hong

Kong for my National Service; off to hitch-hike around Germany; off to India (six times), and Africa (three times). He had even followed my progress when I trained for a charity parachute jump. But on none of those occasions was I driving a double-decker bus on the wrong side of the road. A few days after watching me drive away from his front door he has a heart attack and dies. No-one has ever suggested, at least not to my face, that these two events might be connected, but that thought has been in the back of my mind, nagging me; something I have lived with for over forty years.

Our mother also had a difficult passing. With pains in her stomach she was treated for hiatus hernia when she actually had Barrett's esophagus. Returning to the doctor, she was told "you are old; you must expect to be ill" (she was 76, and had recently wall-papered her staircase and landing). This was when I was working in Scotland: she struggled up there for her annual holiday, and I couldn't believe how much weight she'd lost. She couldn't eat solids and had been living on porridge and soup. I got her to my doctor the next morning: he suspected that the Barrett's esophagus had become cancerous and offered to arrange tests. Mother preferred to do that back in London, nearer to the grandchildren. She had an operation, but was so thin and weak by then that the wall between esophagus and lung was punctured during the operation and didn't recover. She fought on for weeks, but it was always a losing battle.

My parent's ashes share the grave of my paternal grandparents at Ocklynge Cemetery in Eastbourne. An enormous cemetery on a slope of the Downs facing the sun. Thousands of graves and yet, whenever I go to tidy it up or water the plants, I often find myself the only living person in the graveyard - sharing the space with the birds, the squirrels and the butterflies. The French, I believe, handle this much better. Once a year, on All Soul's Day, entire families, entire villages, entire communities make their way to the churchyard wearing Sunday-best and carrying bowls full of brightly-coloured chrysanthemums. More of a carnival than a mourning; they all go off to family lunches leaving the cemetery ablaze with colour, and peopled with happy memories.

Chapter Twenty-Nine: And out to the Rolling Sea.

One more engagement before I headed for Dieppe and the ferry home - but an important one. A talk to the Association France Grande Bretagne about my hero George Bernard Shaw, winner of the Nobel Literature Prize for his play *St Joan*, in the Maid's own city of Orléans. Afternoon tea with another fascinating man, Gerard Hocmard, president of the AFGB, writer, actor - and incredibly helpful with suggestions of future French venues for my talks - and then off to the *Maison des Associations* on the *rue Jeanne d'Arc. Naturellement*; where else would I talk about the author of St Joan?

"Brian Freeland's one-man-show is a great success. His intention is to entertain and inform us on the life of George Bernard Shaw, the writer and philosopher. With the aid of little more than an armchair and a carafe of water, Brian morphs seamlessly from his role as lecturer to that of the great man himself. His English voice transforms into a higher Irish brogue to deliver the bon mots, thoughts and ideas of GBS. The audience was delighted by this performance, which brought the famous Irishman to life before our very eyes. We could almost see the beard". Di Bailey: France Grande Bretagne Association, Orléans.

The viaduct at Rochefort had been the end of my journey of rediscovery down the Charente, but the Charente meanders on for a further thirty kilometres before reaching the open sea. Tidal all the way back to the first lock, at Saint-Savinien, with a drop of over four metres between high and low tides at

Rochefort. As a result slimy alluvial soil is deposited on the banks and has, in times past, blocked the entrances to the dry docks used for the construction of Colbert's navy. One of the very first French steam engines was used to help clear this mud, as were the chained convicts from the penal settlement.

On my last morning in Rochefort I had driven out to the two headlands, four kilometres apart - first crossing the viaduct to Port-des-Barques on the south side of the river, with the tiny Ile Madame just off the coast, and the much larger Ile d'Oléron dominating the view to the west. Back over the viaduct and out to Fouras-les-Bains on the north bank; an attractive little seaside resort with a ferry to the Ile d'Aix, and a distant view of Fort Boyard. That was my last view of the Charente, and a slightly sad one. After a lifetime of usefulness offering opportunities for commerce and pleasure; after serving as a boundary and a route for armies of several nations, and as voyeur to centuries of human history, the Charente is gently absorbed into the mighty Atlantic Ocean.

If any of my readers see this silting up, this running out of steam at the end of a busy working life, as a metaphor for retirement or old age or worse I must insist that was not the intention. It is simply that the two stories - mine and the river's - told in parallel over the preceding pages, have both reached their final chapter. Water from the Charente still flows on - heading for other countries, other continents. For the moment my talks still give me a reason to get up in the morning, delaying for a while longer the ever-present threats of death and daytime television, and offering the hope that I, too, might yet visit more countries, more continents.

Nous verrons.

We'll see.

I leave you with this thought, courtesy of John Galsworthy: the very tenuous personal connection is that it comes from his not-very-good 1915 novel, The Freelands:

"That tragedy of the old - the being laid aside from life before the spirit is ready to resign, the feeling that no-one wants you, that all you have borne and brought up have long passed out onto roads where you cannot follow, that life streams by so fast while you lie up in a backwater, feebly, blindly groping for the full of the water, and always pushed gently, hopelessly back: that sense that you are still young and warm, and yet so furbeloved with old thoughts and fashions that none can see how young and warm you are, none see how you long to rub hearts with the active, how you yearn for something real to do that can help life on, and how no-one will give it to you".

Were it not for the Talks and the Scripts - and the Book - this might well have applied to me.

BIBLIOGRAPHY:

With thanks for helping
to refresh a seventy-seven-
year-old memory bank.

Memoirs of an Egoist
by Badr-Ud-Din Tyabji.
Roli Books PVT.Ltd. New
Delhi 110048

The Shakespeare Wallah
by Geoffrey Kendal and
Clare Colvin.
Penguin

White Cargo
by Felicity Kendal
Penguin

The Prithviwallahs
by Shashi Kapoor and
Deepa Gahlot
Lustre Press/Roli Books.

The Theatres of George Devine
by Irving Wardle.
Jonathan Cape

A Sense of Direction
by William Gaskill.
Faber and Faber

Zefferelli
by Franco Zeffirelli.
Weidenfeld and Nicolson.

PHOTOS:

Courtesy of:
Nottingham Evening Post
Chris Arthur/NT
Khalid Tyabji
Roli Books
Dollar Drama
Jane de Weck
and various French
Bureaux de Tourism

Brian performing GBS:
Playing The Clown

details of all his talks on
www.brianfreeland.co.uk

INDEX:

8

215

NIGERIA 86-87
Ninagawa, Yukio 194-196
Norrington, Roger 133-4
NOTTINGHAM 158-168
Olivier 67-71, 75-76, 122
O'Toole, Peter 25, 98,
            166-168, 183
Palladium 36-40, 42-45.
Pasquale, Joe 136
Perera, Saratchandra 91
Philpotts, Beryl & Don 27
Pick, Prof. John 172-174
PORT d'ENVAUX 187.
Pras, Bernard 63-64.
Pritchard, Mark 174
QATAR 151-154.
Quilley, Denis 120, 135,
            161
Ray, Andrew 90
Raymond, Gary 39, 57.
Richelieu (Cardinal) 92-94
.   201
RICHELIEU 92-101
ROCHEFORT 102,
            196-199, 208-210.
Rota, Nino 71-72
Royal Festival Hall 150-1
RSC (Aldwych) 57-59, 61
Rush, Christopher 176-182
SAINT SAVINIEN 187
SAINT-SIMON 101-102.
SAINTES 156-158
Scofield, Paul 61
Sculpher, David 200, 205
Scottish Opera 132-133
Secombe, Harry 135-136

Shaw, GB 107, 117, 127/9
147, 161, 171, 184, 208
Smith, Maggie 70-71, 73
Spacey, Kevin 181-182
SRI LANKA 90-91
ST MACOUX 29, 40.
Steele, Tommy 43
Stephens, Robert 70, 71
Sterne, Arlene 148
Sumner, John 122
TAILLEBOURG, 185-186
Taylor, Elizabeth 43
Tayside Opera 141-144
Theatre Workshop 59-60
Thorndike, Sybil 74,162/3,
Trinder, Tommy 21, 38-39
Tucker, Sophie 45.
Tully, Sir Mark 108
Tyabji, Badr 108-113
Tyabji, Khalid 112-113
USA   154-156
Vaughan, Frankie 39.
VENISE VERT 202-203
Vergnaud, Marie 40-41
VERTEUIL 45-46
VOULEME 40.
Wardle, Irving 159, 194/6
Washbourne, Mona 89
Weigel, Helene 82
Withers, Googie 121
Wren, Steven 138
Wyckham, John 59, 69
Young, Lee 51
Zeffirelli, Franco 71-72